Weight Wat

Freestyle 2019

The Weight Watchers Freestyle Program 2019 And Recipes That Shape

Your Body and Boost Confidence

ANTHONY JONES

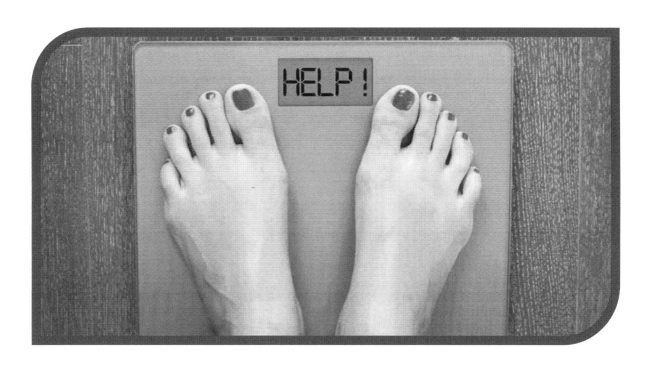

Table of Contents

Weight Watchers 1

Freestyle 2019 1

Introduction 7

The Freestyle program 10

2019 Zero Points Food List 11

Weight Watchers Freestyle Recipes 16

Instant Pot Beef Recipes 16

    6PTS Instant pot Mexican beef 17

    7PTS Maple Smoked Brisket 18

    5PTS Freestyle Spicy Braised Beef 19

    8PTS Tender Beef Bourguignon 20

    6PTS Freestyle Fast Beef Meatballs 21

    7PTS Vegetable Stuffed Peppers with Beef 22

    7PTS Pressure Cooker Pot Roast 23

    8PTS Grain Free Meatballs and Sauce 24

    6PTS Pressure Cooker Texas Red Chili 24

    3PTS Pressure cooked beef ribs 26

    10PTS BBQ Pork Ribs & Bean Salad 26

6PTS Instant Pot Pork Ribs 27

7PTS Pork chops and cabbage 28

5PTS Smothered Pork Chops in the Pot 29

4PTS Flex Cherry Apple Pork Loin 29

5PTS Easy Pork Piccata 30

4PTS Slow Cook Spiced Pulled Pork 30

7PTS Curried Pork Chops 31

6PTS Spicy Pineapple Pork 32

5PTS Green Chile Stew with Pork 33

Instant Pot Chicken Recipes 33

6PTS Whole Chicken in an Instant Pot 34

3PTS Pressure Cooked Chicken Romano 35

4PTS Delicious Shredded Chicken 36

6PTS Freestyle Tasty Orange Chicken 36

6PTS Flex Whole Roasted Chicken 37

8PTS Chicken and Pancetta Risotto 37

10PTS Pineapple Colada Chicken 38

5PTS Pressure Cooker Butter Chicken 39

3PTS One Pot Chicken 40

8PTS Chicken and Vegetable Noodle 40

5PTS Instant Lemon Garlic Chicken 41

7PTS Barbecue Chili Chicken 42

8PTS Cheesy Lemon Chicken 42

10PTS Ultimate Flex Chicken Fajita Pasta 42

2PTS Veggie & Chicken broth 43

7PTS Turkey and Gluten Free Gravy 44

8PFS Turkey Sage Burger 45

5PFS Turkey Strips 45

7PFS Frittata with Turkey Sausage 46

8PFS Turkey Sausage Casserole 46

7PFS Potato Gratin Turkey Sausage 47

9PFS Beef Ragu with Tagliatelle 48

8PFS Tomato Lime Beef Curry 49

10PFS Delicious Beef Stew 50

6PFS Italian Beef Steak Rolls 51

Breakfast Recipes 52

Wake Up Sandwich 52

A delicious and warming breakfast treat 53

Melon Smoothie 53

Whole Wheat Pancakes 54

Morning Power Bar 54

Texan Omelets Wrap 55

Lunch Recipes 56

Pasta & Beans 56

Turkey Reuben 57

The Healthy Roti 57

Sesame Noodles With Chicken 58

Mexican Lunch Minus The Meat 59

Healthy Lunch Pizza 59

Grilled Veggies 60

Dinner Recipes 60

Tex-Mex Burger Wraps 60

Veggie Chili 61

(Makes 6 Servings) Calories per Serving: 210 Lime Chicken 62

Mushroom and Scallion Chicken 62

Broccoli And Shrimp 63

Southwest Steaks w/Salsa Sauce 64

Grilled Eggplant & Portobello Sandwich 65

Deserts Recipes 65

Fruity Parfaits 65

Mocha Pudding 66

Banana Quesadillas 66

Broiled Mango 67

Sesame Squares 67

Easy Chocolate Cake 68

Grapefruit Mango Sorbet 68

The Bonus 7 Step Action 112

1.The Ultimate weight loss program 112

3. Persistent 116

4. Find A Good Partner 117

4. Tracking Results 117

5. Eating Clean 118

6. How Much Should You Eat? 119

7. Positive Image 120

Activities Workout Routine 121

Conclusion 128

Soup Recipes 72

Salad and Side Dish Recipes 92

Slow Cooker Beef and Barbeque 103

Slow Cooker Stew 104

Slow Cooker Tacos 105

Mushrooms and Beef Noodles 106

Beef Ragu Style 106

Lasagna Beef 108

Beef Chili 109

Beef Stroganoff 110

Beef Burgundy 110

Introduction

If you've been trying diet after diet to lose weight, only to have those extra pounds stay stubbornly in place, it's time to try a new approach. The truth is that there's no secret diet that's going to burn away fat. What you need to do is make a few changes to the way you eat and Make those changes a long term habit. That is, you have to nourish your body and feed it what it really needs in order to lose weight.

For normal functioning of the body, we need essential nutrients like carbohydrates, fats, vitamins, proteins and minerals. These nutrients are generally sourced from plants and animal foods. We burn a significant amount of energy in our daily activities. If not refilled, we find it harder to concentrate on work and feel exhausted or frustrated.

The Weight Watchers diet is the only diet that allows you to eat anything you want like ice cream, pasta, cheese, and all other favorite things while enabling you to lose weight. When following this diet, you'll learn how you can become healthier without sacrificing your love for food.

With this diet program, you'll learn how to create healthier food without taking away so much from the taste department.

In the this book, you'll learn how you can cook flavorful soup, fulfilling main dishes, yummy salad and side dishes, loaded breakfast and appetizers, and delicious desserts.

The Weight Watchers diet prevents you from taking in empty calories without worrying too much on what you eat. It takes minimal effort to follow this diet as all you have to do is to follow the recipes I've included in this book. If you want to take the diet to the next level, you can also search online for personalized activity goals to help you reach your weight goals faster.

Aside from exercise and diet plans, you can also find communities online who can give you advice and tips so you can also be successful in this diet. Let get your family join in on the fun as this diet is good for everybody.

People with high cholesterol, diabetes, high blood pressure, and heart disease will greatly benefit from this diet as it helps you maintain healthy levels of food nutrition to prevent complications caused by improper diet. If you're not too sure, you can always check with your doctor whether this type of diet will affect your health.

Next, we have created the ultimate seven days complete weight loss program, if you follow correctly it will 100% drastically melting your fat away in 7 days. We don't promise you every answer, but we do know that if you incorporate these tips into your lifestyle you will be healthier. We also know that if you do want to lose weight these lessons can be life changing.

At the end of the book, you will learn more than a hundred Weight Watchers recipes that you can use to spice up your meal plan or to entice a loved one to join you in this healthier food lifestyle.

The Freestyle program

Based on the successful SmartPoints® system, WW Freestyle offers more than 200 zero Points® foods—including eggs, skinless chicken breast, fish and seafood, corn, beans, peas, and so much more—to multiply your meal and menu possibilities. And it makes life simpler, too: You can forget about weighing, measuring, or tracking those zero Points foods.

Total flexibility

And because we recognize that every day is different—and some days are *really* different (think parties, business travel, holiday open houses....)—we've made your SmartPoints Budget more flexible than ever. Up to 4 unused daily SmartPoints can now roll over into your weekly SmartPoints to give you a bigger "bank" to use whenever and however you like.

How It Works

- For those of you not already familiar with SmartPoints, the SmartPoints system uses the latest nutritional science to make healthy eating as simple as possible. It nudges you toward making healthy choices so eat better and lose weight.
- Every food and drink has a SmartPoints value: a number that is based on calories, protein, sugar and saturated fat. The baseline SmartPoints value is based on the food's calories. Protein lowers the SmartPoints value. Saturated fat and sugar increase the SmartPoints value.
- Every day you get a SmartPoints Budget to spend on any foods you want.
- Your Daily SmartPoints Budget is calculated based on your age, height, weight and gender with a minimum daily value of 23.
- You only need to track the foods that have a SmartPoints value.
- You don't need to weigh, measure or track 0 SmartPoints foods.
- Enjoy a greatly total list of 0 SmartPoints go-to foods at the end of this book.
- Every week you also get a Weekly SmartPoints Budget that you can think of as "overdraft" protection. They are there to use when you go over your Daily SmartPoints budget.
- You can roll over up to four (4) unused Daily SmartPoints into your Weekly SmartPoints. Use them or not as you see fit.

Rollover Points

With the new Weight Watchers Freestyle plan for 2019, you will be able to roll over up to 4 SmartPoints daily if you do not use them.

I love this idea since it means you could adjust your points to match the natural rhythms and fluctuations of your appetite.

Here are some of the latest recipes available so you can try out the Freestyle program

2019 Zero Points Food List

- Zero Point Foods
- Instead of counting calories, Weight Watchers uses a point system to help control what you eat to lose weight. A mathematical equation focused on saturated fat, sugar, carb and calorie content is used to determine the point value for a food. Zero point foods are low in all these categories. All fresh fruit and most vegetables have zero points, with the exception of starchy vegetables such as corn or potatoes. In addition to helping fill you up without costing you any points, the list is used to help dieters on the Weight Watchers program make healthier food choices.

-

- Nonstarchy Veggies
- People who eat more vegetables tend to weigh less. Veggies are low in calories and high in fiber, so they fill you up without making too much of an impact on your calorie intake. Any nonstarchy vegetable is a zero point food. These include broccoli, cauliflower, carrots, cucumbers, peppers, onions, snow peas, zucchini, greens and lettuce. When you feel a little hungry while following the Weight Watchers diet, you can make yourself a salad and enjoy it without having to worry about points.
- All Kinds of Fruit
- As with veggies, eating more fruit might help you weigh less. Although not as low in calories as nonstarchy vegetables, fruit is still lower in calories than a cookie or an ice cream cone, and it's more nutritious too. Any fresh fruit, even those banned from other diets such as grapes and bananas, have zero points on the Weight Watchers plan. Apples, oranges, strawberries, kiwi, watermelon and pears have zero points. Eating these healthy foods satisfies your taste buds and your appetite. Add sliced strawberries to your zero point salad for a touch of sweetness.
- Food Flavorings and Special Treats
- You can flavor your food without feeling guilty with a number of different items on the zero point list, such as vinegar, lemon or lime juice, hot sauce, ketchup, mustard, salsa and soy sauce. Drizzle a little vinegar on your salad to complete your zero point snack.
- Broth, which you can sip on a cold day to keep you warm and satisfy your craving for something savory, is also a zero point food. You can consume sugar-free ice pops, diet soda and sugar-free gelatin without sacrificing any of your points as well.

200+ Zero Points Foods

- Here it is: an expanded list of all 200+ zero Points foods. The foods on this list form the foundation of a healthy eating pattern, so you don't need to weigh, measure, or track any of them
- Apples
- Applesauce, unsweetened
- Apricots
- Arrowroot
- Artichoke hearts
- Artichokes
- Arugula
- Asparagus

- Bamboo shoots
- Banana
- Beans: including adzuki, black, broad (fava), butter, cannellini, cranberry (Roman), green, garbanzo (chickpeas), great northern, kidney, lima, lupini, mung, navy, pink, pinto, small white, snap, soy, string, wax, white
- Beans, refried, fat-free, canned
- Beets
- Berries, mixed
- Blackberries
- Blueberries
- Broccoli
- Broccoli rabe
- Broccoli slaw
- Broccolini
- Brussels sprouts

- Cabbage: all varieties including Chinese (bok choy), Japanese, green, red, napa, savory, pickled
- Calamari, grilled
- Cantaloupe
- Carrots
- Cauliflower
- Caviar
- Celery
- Swiss chard
- Cherries
- Chicken breast, ground, 99% fat-free
- Chicken breast or tenderloin, skinless, boneless or with bone
- Clementines
- Coleslaw mix (shredded cabbage and carrots), packaged
- Collards
- Corn, baby (ears), white, yellow, kernels, on the cob
- Cranberries
- Cucumber

- Daikon
- Dates, fresh
- Dragon fruit

- Edamame, in pods or shelled

- Egg substitutes
- Egg whites
- Eggplant
- Eggs, whole, including yolks
- Endive
- Escarole

- Fennel (anise, sweet anise, or finocchio)
- Figs
- Fish: anchovies, arctic char, bluefish, branzino (sea bass), butterfish, carp, catfish, cod, drum, eel, flounder, grouper, haddock, halibut, herring, mackerel, mahimahi (dolphinfish), monkfish, orange roughy, perch, pike, pollack, pompano, rainbow trout (steelhead), rockfish, roe, sablefish (including smoked), salmon (all varieties), salmon, smoked (lox), sardines, sea bass, smelt, snapper, sole, striped bass, striped mullet, sturgeon (including smoked); white sucker, sunfish (pumpkinseed), swordfish, tilapia, tilefish, tuna (all varieties), turbot, whitefish (including smoked), whitefish and pike (store-bought), whiting
- Fish fillet, grilled with lemon pepper
- Fruit cocktail
- Fruit cup, unsweetened
- Fruit salad
- Fruit, unsweetened

- Garlic
- Ginger root
- Grapefruit
- Grapes
- Greens: beet, collard, dandelion, kale, mustard, turnip
- Greens, mixed baby
- Guavas
- Guavas, strawberry

- Hearts of palm (palmetto)
- Honeydew melon
- Jackfruit
- Jerk chicken breast
- Jerusalem artichokes (sunchokes)
- Jicama (yam bean)

- Kiwifruit
- Kohlrabi
- Kumquats

- Leeks
- Lemon
- Lemon zest
- Lentils
- Lettuce, all varieties
- Lime
- Lime zest

- Litchis (lychees)

- Mangoes
- Melon balls
- Mung bean sprouts
- Mung dal
- Mushroom caps
- Mushrooms: all varieties including brown, button, crimini, Italian, portabella, shiitake

- Nectarine
- Nori seaweed

- Okra
- Onions
- Oranges: all varieties including blood

- Papayas
- Parsley
- Passion fruit
- Pea shoots
- Peaches
- Peapods, black-eye
- Pears
- Peas and carrots
- Peas: black-eyed, chickpeas (garbanzo), cowpeas (blackeyes, crowder, southern), young pods with seeds, green, pigeon, snow (Chinese pea pods); split, sugar snap
- Peppers, all varieties
- Pepperoncini
- Persimmons
- Pickles, unsweetened
- Pico de gallo
- Pimientos, canned
- Pineapple
- Plumcots (pluots)
- Plums
- Pomegranate seeds
- Pomegranates
- Pomelo (pummelo)
- Pumpkin
- Pumpkin puree

- Radicchio
- Radishes
- Raspberries
- Rutabagas

- Salad, mixed greens
- Salad, side, without dressing, fast food
- Salad, three-bean
- Salad, tossed, without dressing
- Salsa verde
- Salsa, fat free

- Salsa, fat free; gluten-free
- Sashimi
- Satay, chicken, without peanut sauce
- Satsuma mandarin
- Sauerkraut
- Scallions
- Seaweed
- Shallots
- Shellfish: abalone, clams, crab (including Alaska king, blue, dungeness, lump crabmeat, queen) crayfish, cuttlefish, lobster (including spiny lobster), mussels, octopus, oysters, scallops, shrimp, squid
- Spinach
- Sprouts, including alfalfa, bean, lentil
- Squash, summer (all varieties including zucchini)
- Squash, winter (all varieties including spaghetti)
- Starfruit (carambola)
- Strawberries
- Succotash

- Tangelo
- Tangerine
- Taro
- Tofu, all varieties
- Tofu, smoked
- Tomatillos
- Tomato puree
- Tomato sauce
- Tomatoes: all varieties including plum, grape, cherry
- Turkey breast, ground, 99% fat-free
- Turkey breast or tenderloin, skinless, boneless or with bone
- Turkey breast, skinless, smoked
- Turnips
  Vegetable sticks
- Vegetables, mixed
- Vegetables, stir fry, without sauce

- Water chestnuts
- Watercress
- Watermelon

- Yogurt, Greek, plain, nonfat, unsweetened
- Yogurt, plain, nonfat, unsweetened
- Yogurt, soy, plain

Weight Watchers Freestyle Recipes
Instant Pot Beef Recipes

6PTS Instant pot Mexican beef

Ready in 50 minutes,

6 servings

Freestyle Points value per serving: 6

Ingredients

- 3 pounds' boneless beef short ribs sliced into cubes
- ½ cup chili powder
- 2 teaspoons salt
- 1 tablespoon fat
- 1 medium onion, thinly sliced
- 2 tablespoon tomato paste
- 5 garlic cloves, well peeled and smashed
- ½ cup roasted tomato salsa
- ½-1 cup bone broth
- 1 teaspoon Red Boat Fish Sauce
- black pepper, freshly ground
- ½ cup minced cilantro
- 2 radishes, thinly sliced

Instructions

1. Combine the cubed beef, chili powder, and salt in a large bowl.
2. Bring pot to medium heat and when the fat melts, add the onions then sauté until soft.
3. Stir in tomato paste and garlic, and cook until fragrant or 30 seconds.
4. Add in the seasoned beef then pour in the salsa, fish sauce and stock.
5. Tight lid the pot and cook on high heat until high pressure is reached. Afterwards, lower the heat to maintain high pressure for about 30 minutes. Release pressure naturally for 15 minutes.
6. Unlock the lid, season with salt and pepper to taste and serve.

Nutrition information

Calories: 209.5

Carbohydrates: 6.8g

Fats: 13.4g

Proteins: 15.1g

7PTS Maple Smoked Brisket

Ready in 1 hr. 30 minutes

8 servings

Freestyle Points value per serving: 7

Ingredients

- 1 lb. beef brisket
- 1-2 tablespoons maple, date, or coconut sugar,
- 2 teaspoons sea salt, smoked
- 1 teaspoon black pepper
- 1 teaspoon mustard powder
- 1 teaspoon onion powder
- ½ teaspoon smoked paprika
- 2 cups bone broth
- 3 fresh thyme sprigs

Instructions

1. Withdraw the brisket from refrigerator 30 minutes before cooking. Dry it with paper towels and set aside.
2. Combine the maple sugar, pepper, smoked sea salt, onion powder, mustard powder, and smoked paprika.Coat the meat with the mixture on all sides.
3. Add to the Instant Pot and allow it to fry for 2-3 minutes until golden brown. Turn the brisket and add the broth, thyme and liquid smoke. Scrape any browned bits at the bottom and then cover with the lid.
4. Allow to cook for 50 minutes and release steam naturally. Withdraw the brisket from the pot cover with foil and set aside. Slice the brisket and serve it.

Nutrition information

Calories: 542.9

Carbohydrates: 30.3g

Fats: 24g

Proteins: 45.6g

5PTS Freestyle Spicy Braised Beef

Time: 90 mins

Number of servings: 4

Freestyle Points value per serving: 5

Ingredients:

- Two pounds chopped into 3-inch pieces eye of round beef, without fat four cloves garlic half of medium onion Juice of one lime.
- Two tbsps. chipotles in adobo sauce
- One tbsp. ground oregano
- One tbsp. ground cumin
- One cup water
- Two tsp kosher salt
- Three bay leaves
- One tsp olive oil
- Pinch of ground cloves
- Black pepper to taste

Directions:

• Season the beef with salt and pepper. Pour oil into your Instant Pot, place meat and select "Sauté" function. Cook meat until it's browned.

• Blend lime juice, onion, garlic, water, chipotle, oregano, and cloves in your blender.

• Pour that blended mixture into the pot and mix bay leaves. Select "Manual" function to cook on high pressure for one hour.

• Use natural pressure release method.

• Remove the meat from the pot then shred it. And mix this shredded beef with cooking liquid.

• Serve and enjoy!

8PTS Tender Beef Bourguignon

Ready in 1 hour,

6 servings

Freestyle Points value per serving: 8

Ingredients

- 4-6 strips smoked bacon, chopped
- 2 lbs. chuck beef sliced
- 6 tablespoons flour, all purpose
- 1 tablespoon sea salt
- ½ teaspoon black pepper
- 3 tablespoon butter
- 1 lb. carrots, cut into thin chunks
- 5 garlic cloves, chopped
- 2 sliced yellow onions
- 1 lb. quartered fresh mushrooms
- 1 bay leaf
- 1 teaspoon fresh thyme leaves
- 3-4 cups red wine
- 2 cups stock or beef broth
- 1 tablespoon tomato paste

Instructions

1. Make Marinade. Dry the beef with paper towel.
2. Marinade the meat in 4 cups of red wine, salt and pepper. Allow to stay overnight.
3. Drain the beef but keep the wine, dry the beef with a paper towel and put the chunks in a bowl. Coat all sides generously with flour, salt, and pepper, set aside.
4. On the Instant Pot select "Saute" and add in the chopped bacon and the meat pieces. If possible, cook the in batches. Afterwards, withdraw them and set aside.
5. Melt the butter and add carrots, garlic and onions. Sauté until onions are softened. Add in mushrooms and sauté for a minute.
6. Add the reserved wine, thyme and bay leaf. Allow to 'simmer' for about 3 minutes. Add in the beef, beef broth and tomato paste. Stir well.
7. Tightly close with lid and ensure the vent valve is closed. Select MEAT setting (30 minutes). Add any remaining flour to butter to make a roux.
8. Let the pressure release naturally and add the roux to thicken the sauce. Serve over any carb

Nutrition information

Calories: 461

Carbohydrates: 12g

Fats: 18g

Proteins: 49g

6PTS Freestyle Fast Beef Meatballs

Time: 20 mins

Number of servings: 4

Freestyle Points per serving: 6

Ingredients:

- One pound ground beef
- Two crumbled bread slices
- Two chopped carrots
- Two cups pasta sauce
- Two cups water
- One chopped onion
- One beaten egg
- Half tsp garlic salt
- Salt and pepper to taste

Directions:

1. Take a mixing bowl and mix ground beef, egg, crumbled bread, onion, carrots, garlic salt, salt, and pepper.
2. Make meatballs from that mixture and set them aside.
3. Pour water and pasta sauce into your Instant Pot and stir well.
4. One by one add meatballs in the pasta sauce mixture.
5. Seal pot with the lid, select "Manual" and cook on high pressure for five minutes.
6. Allow release pressure naturally.
7. Serve meatballs with pasta, rice, and enjoy!

7PTS Vegetable Stuffed Peppers with Beef

Time: 30 mins

Number of servings: 4

Freestyle Points per serving: 7

Ingredients:

- One pound ground beef
- One cup brown rice
- Four bell peppers
- One diced tomato
- One can tomato sauce
- One egg
- One chopped onion
- One cup shredded mozzarella cheese
- Half tsp dried parsley
- Half tsp garlic powder
- Half tsp oregano
- Salt and pepper to taste

Directions:

1. Take a mixing bowl and mix ground beef, rice, egg, tomato, onion, parsley, oregano, salt, and pepper.
2. Slice off the bell peppers tops. Then stuff meat mixture into the bell peppers.
3. Pour water and half of tomato sauce in your Instant Pot. Then place a trivet in the pot and place stuffed peppers on top.

4. Now pour all remaining tomato sauce over the top of peppers.
5. Seal the pot with the lid and select "Manual" function for fifteen minutes.
6. Use natural pressure release. Open the lid carefully and add mozzarella cheese on the top of peppers.
7. Close the lid again just for a few seconds, until cheese melted.
8. Serve immediately and enjoy!

7PTS Pressure Cooker Pot Roast

Ready in 1 hr. 45 minutes,

6 servings

Freestyle Points value per serving: 7

Ingredients

- 3 lbs. boneless chuck roast
- 1/2 tablespoon ghee
- 1/2 teaspoon black pepper
- 1/2 teaspoon salt
- 1 yellow onion, chopped
- 2 clove garlics, minced
- 1 tablespoon tomato paste
- 2 cups beef broth
- 1 cup chicken broth
- 1/4 cup red wine
- 1 tablespoon Worcestershire sauce
- 2 lbs. red potatoes, sliced into thin chunks
- 2 lbs. carrots, chopped
- 5-6oz white mushrooms, sliced in half
- salt and pepper

Instructions:

1. Season the roast with salt and pepper. Add in the ghee to the instant pot and fry for about 2 minutes and then add the roast. Allow all sides to brown for about 6 minutes each
2. Withdraw the roast and put aside. Add in the onion and fry for about 4 minutes until softened and stir often then add the garlic and tomato paste, stir together for 30 seconds until aromatic.
3. Add in the broths, wine, and Worcestershire sauce. Combine well by stirring and bring to a simmer. Add the roast and any juices.

4. Cover the pot and set it on high pressure for 45 minutes. Once finished. Afterwards, release pressure naturally.
5. Withdraw the lid and transfer the roast to a baking sheet, set aside.
6. Add the potatoes, mushrooms and carrots to the Instant Pot, cover with the lid, and bring pressure to high for 6 minutes. Meanwhile, transfer the roast to the oven and broil for 4 minutes, remove again and transfer it to a cutting board.
7. Release pressure form Instant Pot once the vegetables are cooked. Transfer the vegetables to the baking sheet using a slotted spoon.
8. Place the vegetables in the oven and then broil for 5 minutes until browned. Slice the roast and place it on a platter and add the vegetables to the same platter. Pour some of the simmered liquid over the roast and vegetables. Serve immediately with the sauce.

Nutrition information

Calories: 256, Carbohydrates: 1g, Fats: 16g, Proteins: 25g

8PTS Grain Free Meatballs and Sauce

Ready in 3-4 hours,

8-10 servings

Freestyle Points value per serving: 8

Ingredients:

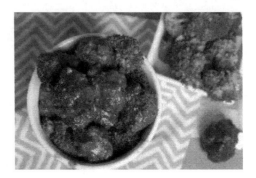

- 2 eggs
- pound organic beef, ground
- 4-5 tablespoons, fruit-sweetened grape jelly
- 1/2 cup , organic
- 1/2 teaspoon pepper, ground
- 1/2 teaspoon Spanish paprika
- 1/4 teaspoon chili powder
- 1 teaspoon ground garlic salt
- 1/4 cup tapioca flour or arrowroot

Instructions

1. Heat oven to about 350
2. Combine the beef, pepper, eggs, garlic salt and tapioca starch in a mixing bowl
3. Make small golf ball sized meatballs with the mixture and transfer to a baking sheet
4. Bake until browned or about 25 minutes.
5. Transfer the baked meatballs to crockpot, add chili sauce, paprika, grape jelly, and chili powder.
6. Cook on low heat for 2-4 hours, occasionally checking. Serve with any of your favorite greens or over rice.
7. NOTE: When an Instant Pot is used, you don't have to bake the meatballs in advance.

Nutrition information

Calories: 291.2

Carbohydrates: 33.6g

Fats: 9.5g

Proteins: 19.4g

6PTS Pressure Cooker Texas Red Chili

Ready in 1 hour, 6 servings,

Freestyle Points value per serving: 6

Ingredients

- 1 tablespoon vegetable oil
- 4-5 pounds' beef chuck roast, chopped 2 inch cubes
- ½ tablespoon kosher salt
- 2 onions, diced
- 3 cloves garlic, minced
- 2 minced chipotles with sauce
- 1/2 teaspoon kosher salt
- 1 teaspoon chili powder
- ½ cup cumin
- 2 teaspoons Mexican oregano
- 1 cup coffee
- 14 ounces can of crushed tomatoes
- Salt and pepper to taste

Instructions

1. Brown the beef: Heat the oil in the cooker pot over medium-high heat for 30 seconds. Sprinkle the beef with salt and then brown in two to three batches. Brown each batch on one side, about five minutes.
2. Add in the onions and 1/2 teaspoon of kosher salt to the cooker. Fry the onions for about 5 minutes until softened while scraping with a spoon to remove any stuck bits on the bottom. Add the garlic cloves and chipotle and then fry for one minute. Add the chili powder, oregano and cumin. Allow to cook for one minute and then stir the spices into the onions.
3. Pour the beef and any juices into the cooker, and then add the crushed tomatoes. Stir until the beef is completely coated in tomatoes and spices.
4. Shut the cooker tightly, bring the high heat and maximum pressure. Cook for 25 minutes and then release pressure naturally, about 15 minutes and then remove the lid.
5. Add salt to reduce chili bitterness. Serve the chili straight up.

Nutrition information

Calories: 225

Carbohydrates: 7g

Fats: 16g

Proteins: 14g

3PTS Pressure cooked beef ribs

Ready in 25-30 minutes,

2 servings

Freestyle Points value per serving: 3

Ingredients

- 1 rack of beef back ribs
- Dry rub
- ½ cup kosher salt
- ½ cup water
- 4 ounces of applesauce, unsweetened
- 2 tablespoons coconut oil
- 1 teaspoon fish sauce

Instructions

1. Dry the beef back ribs with a paper towel and then, sprinkle with the dry rub and salt. Wrap up in foil and set aside to marinate for two hours.
2. Preheat the broiler, grab the rack from the fridge and cut to fit in the pressure cooker. Put the ribs on a wire rack in a baking sheet rimmed and foil lined.
3. Broil the ribs for 1-2 minutes each side. Add water, fish sauce applesauce and coconut oil to the pressure cooker and stir to combine, add a rack to the pot.
4. Put the ribs into the cooker and tight lid. Bring the heat to high pressure and lower to maintain high pressure. Cook for 20 minutes and release pressure naturally and quickly.
5. Withdraw the ribs and place them back on a wire rack lined with foil and rimmed baking sheet.
6. Simmer the remaining cooking liquid for 5 minutes and skim off any excess fat and adjust seasoning.
7. Coat the racks with the remaining liquid and broil them for one minute.

Nutrition information

Calories: 87

Carbohydrates: 0g

Fats: 7g

Proteins: 4.7g

Instant Pot Pork Recipes

10PTS BBQ Pork Ribs & Bean Salad

Ready in 45 minutes, 6 servings,

Freestyle Points value per serving: 10

Ingredients

- 2 pounds' baby back pork ribs
- 1 cup ready barbecue sauce
- 1 pinch salt
- 1 pinch black pepper freshly ground
- 1 tablespoon olive oil
- 1 yellow onion, diced

- 2 cups water
- 1 cup dried cannellini beans, soaked, well rinsed, and drained
- 1 bay leaf
- 1 garlic clove, chopped
- 6 ounces' fresh spinach

Instructions

1. Cut the ribs and coat them with the barbecue sauce. Sprinkle with salt and pepper. Keep the remaining sauce aside and arrange the ribs in a steamer basket. Set aside.
2. Bring the pressure cooker base to medium heat, add oil, and heat briefly. Add and stir in the onion and sauté until softened, or for about 4 minutes. Add in the water, beans, and bay leaf, stir.
3. Lower the steamer basket into the pressure cooker, close and lock the lid. Bring pressure to high pressure and cook for 20 minutes. When the cooking time is up, open the pressure cooker with the usual Natural Release method for 10 minutes.
4. Carefully withdraw the steamer basket from the cooker and cover with aluminum foil. Discard the bay leaf from the beans, mix in 1 teaspoon salt, the garlic, and spinach. Scoop the bean mixture into a large casserole using a spoon. Arrange the ribs on top of the beans and brush with the spared barbecue sauce.
5. Broil the casserole for 3 to 5 minutes until the sauce on the ribs is lightly caramelize. Serve immediately.

Nutrition information

Calories: 572, Carbohydrates: 18.7g

Fats: 39.5g

Proteins: 33.6gg

6PTS Instant Pot Pork Ribs

Ready in 40 minutes,

3 servings

Freestyle Points value per serving: 6

Ingredients

- 1 Rack Pork Ribs
- ½ Large Onion, Sliced
- 2 Garlic cloves, minced
- 2 Bottles Ray's Honey Chipotle Sauce
- 1 teaspoon Sea Salt
- ½ teaspoon Pepper
- 2 tablespoons arrowroot Powder

Instructions

1. Add in the onion and garlic into the Instant Pot. Pour half of the sauce over the onions. Cut the ribs and layer on top of the onion and garlic. Generously season with salt & Pepper. Pour remaining sauce over the ribs.
2. Tightly cover with lid and close pressure valve. Select the meat setting and increase time to 35 minutes. Allow to cook until timer goes off.
3. Release the steam, remove the ribs and transfer to a plate and cover with foil

4. Click fry button to bring the sauce a boil quickly. Mix 2 teaspoons of arrowroot powder in about ¼ cup of water and stir well. Pour gently into the sauce while stirring. Add the remainder of the mixture if more thickening is needed. Turn the Instant Pot off and serve.

Nutrition information

Calories: 234

Carbohydrates: 0g

Fats: 18g

Proteins: 18g

7PTS Pork chops and cabbage

Ready in 20 minutes

4 servings

Freestyle Points value per serving: 7

Ingredients

- 4 pork chops, thick cut
- 1-2 teaspoon of fennel seeds
- ½ tablespoon salt
- 1 teaspoon pepper
- 1 small head of cabbage
- ¾ cup meat stock
- 1 tablespoon vegetable oil
- 2 teaspoons flour

Instructions

1. Sprinkle the pork chops with fennel, pepper and salt.
2. Slicing the cabbage into half, and then into thick ¾ inch slices then set aside.
3. Heat oil to the pre-heated pressure cooker over medium-high heat and brown all the chops and then set aside. Afterwards, add in the cabbage slices to the empty pressure cooker.
4. Arrange the pork chops on top of the cabbage brown-side up. Add in any juice from the chops.
5. Cover the cooker with lid and bring pressure to high heat and pressure. Turn up the heat high and then lower to maintain pressure. Cook for the next 6-8 minutes at high pressure.
6. Afterwards, open the cooker gently by slowly releasing the pressure.
7. Extract the cabbage and pork chops onto a serving platter. Bring the remaining juices in the pressure cooker to boil and then whisk-in the flour.
8. Pour the thickened sauce on the cabbage and pork chops platter and then serve.

Nutrition information

Calories: 366

Carbohydrates: 22g

Fats: 22g

Proteins: 20g

5PTS Smothered Pork Chops in the Pot

Ready in 30 minutes,

4 servings

Freestyle Points value per serving: 5

Ingredients

- 4 bone in pork chops
- salt and pepper
- 2 bacon fats, tallow, coconut oil
- 1 large onion minced
- 3 cloves garlic, minced
- 1 tsp. dried tarragon or thyme
- 4 oz.sliced ham
- 2 cups broth
- 2 bay leaves
- 1 parsley, chopped
- 3 arrowroots
- ½ cup milk or coconut milk

Instructions

1. Sauté the chops on both sides in the fat and transfer onto on a plate.
2. Add in the onions and some more fat, sauté for 5 minutes until translucent.
3. Add in the garlic and tarragon then sauté until the garlic is fragrant.
4. Add the sliced bacon or ham and sauté until well heated through then add the broth and bay leaves. Switch off the sauté feature and return pork chops into the pot.
5. Close with the lid and select the meat/stew feature to shorten cooking time to around 20 minutes. Afterwards, release the steam and carefully remove the lid. Turn the sauté feature on and then transfer the chops onto a platter. Set aside.
6. Mix the arrowroot with the milk and add to the pot mixture, stirring with a whisk to make the gravy consistent enough. Serve with cauliflower rice

Nutrition information

Calories: 208

Carbohydrates: 10.5g

Fats: 4.4g

Proteins: 29.6g

4PTS Flex Cherry Apple Pork Loin

Total Time: 50 mins

Number of servings: 4

Freestyle Points per serving: 4

Ingredients:

- One and a half pound boneless pork loin
- Two cups chopped apple

- Half cup apple juice
- Half cup pitted cherry
- Half cup chopped onion
- Half cup chopped celery
- One tbsp olive oil
- Salt and pepper to taste

Directions:

• Mix all ingredients in your Instant Pot and close the lid.

• Select "Meat/Stew" function, and cook for forty minutes.

• Use quick pressure release method.

• Serve and enjoy!

5PTS Easy Pork Piccata

Serves: 4

Freestyle Points value per serving: 5

Ingredients:

1 pound pork medallions

1 tablespoon olive oil or cooking spray

½ teaspoon salt

1 teaspoon black pepper

2 cloves garlic, crushed and minced

2 tablespoon capers

¼ cup dry vermouth

¼ cup fresh lemon juice

1 tablespoon fresh chives for garnish (optional)

Directions:

1. Heat the olive oil or cooking spray in a skillet over medium heat.
2. Arrange the pork medallions in the skillet and season with salt and black pepper. Cook for 2-3 minutes per side, or until cooked through.
3. Remove the pork medallions from the heat and keep warm until ready to serve.
4. Add the garlic and capers to the skillet. Cook for 1 minute, stirring gently.
5. Add the vermouth and lemon juice. Continue to cook while stirring and scraping the pan for 1-2 minutes.
6. Remove the sauce from the heat and immediately pour it over the pork medallions for serving.
7. Serve garnished with fresh chives, if desired.

Nutritional Information:

Calories 252, Total Fat 9.4 g, Saturated Fat 2.4 g, Total Carbohydrate 0.2 g, Dietary Fiber 0.1 g, Sugars 0.0 g, Protein 33.4 g

4PTS Slow Cook Spiced Pulled Pork

Serves 6

Freestyle Points value per serving: 4

Ingredients

Rub

- 1 tablespoon paprika
- 1-3 teaspoons ancho chili powder according to taste
- 1 teaspoon salt
- 1 teaspoon ground cumin
- 1 teaspoon dry oregano
- ½ teaspoon black pepper
- ¼ teaspoon cinnamon
- ¼ teaspoon dry coriander

Other ingredients

- 2 pounds pork tenderloin, trimmed
- 1 onion, diced
- 4 garlic cloves, minced
- 1 cup low fat beef broth
- 1 tablespoon apple cider vinegar

Directions

1. Mix together all the rub ingredients in a small bowl.
2. Rub the spice mix all over the pork
3. Place the garlic, onion, beef broth and apple cider vinegar in the slow cooker. Stir a few times to mix well.
4. Add the pork.
5. Set on LOW and cook for 4-6 hours until the pork is cooked through and shred easily with a fork.

Nutritional Information:

Calories 190, Total Fat 4.3 g, Saturated Fat 1.2 g, Total Carbohydrate 5.4 g, Dietary Fiber 1.1 g, Sugars 0.9 g, Protein 32.8 g

7PTS Curried Pork Chops

Serves: 4,

Freestyle Points value per serving: 7

Ingredients:

- 1 pound boneless pork chops, approximately ¼ inch thick
- Cooking spray
- 1 teaspoon salt
- 1 teaspoon black pepper

- 2 ½ cups carrots, sliced
- 1 cup unsweetened coconut milk
- 1 ½ tablespoon curry powder
- 1 teaspoon lime zest
- Cooked rice for serving, optional

Directions:

1. Preheat the oven to 450°F and spray an 8x8 or larger baking dish with cooking spray.
2. Season the pork with salt and black pepper.
3. Place the pork and the sliced carrots in the baking dish, spreading them out into as even a layer as possible.
4. In a bowl, combine the coconut milk, curry powder, and lime zest. Mix well and pour over the pork.
5. Place the baking dish in the oven and bake for 25-30 minutes, or until the pork is cooked through and the carrots are tender.
6. Remove from the oven and let it rest for several minutes before serving.
7. Serve with cooked rice, if desired.

Nutritional Information:

Calories 367, Total Fat 20.1 g, Saturated Fat 7.5 g, Total Carbohydrate 9.9 g, Dietary Fiber 2.2 g, Sugars 3.4 g, Protein 34.9 g

6PTS Spicy Pineapple Pork

Serves: 4

Freestyle Points value per serving: 6

Ingredients:

- 1 pound cooked pork, shredded
- 1 tablespoon vegetable oil or cooking spray
- 3 cups broccoli florets
- 1 teaspoon salt
- 1 teaspoon black pepper
- 2 cups medium heat tomato salsa, fresh or jarred
- 2 cups fresh pineapple chunks
- ¼ cup fresh orange juice (or other citrus juice of choice)
- Fresh cilantro for serving (optional)
- Cooked rice for serving (optional)

Directions:

1. Heat the vegetable oil or cooking spray in a large skillet over medium heat.
2. Add the broccoli and sauté for 5-7 minutes, or until crisp tender.
3. Add the shredded pork to the skillet and season with salt and black pepper.
4. Next, add the salsa, pineapple chunks, and orange juice. Mix well.
5. Increase the heat to medium high until the liquid comes to a low boil.
6. Reduce the heat to low, cover, and simmer for 5-7 minutes, or until heated through.
7. Remove from the heat and serve with cooked rice and cilantro, if desired.

Nutritional Information:

Calories 328, Total Fat 10.3 g, Saturated Fat 2.5 g, Total Carbohydrate 22.7 g, Dietary Fiber 5.0 g, Sugars 9.4 g, Protein 37.4 g

5PTS Green Chile Stew with Pork

Total Time: 30 mins

Number of servings: 4

Freestyle Points per serving: 5

Ingredients:

- One pound chopped into bite-sized pork sirloin tip roast
- One pound chopped sweet potato
- Half 7-oz can of diced chilies
- One cup chopped fresh tomatoes
- One cup chicken broth
- One can of drained black beans
- One cup chopped onion
- Half cup chopped cilantro
- One tbsp. Italian seasoning
- Half tbsp. chili powder
- One tbsp. yogurt
- One tsp avocado oil
- Salt and pepper to taste

Directions:

• Season meat with salt and pepper. Pour avocado oil in your Instant Pot. Then add meat and select "Sauté" function.

• Now add chilies, chili powder, onion, Italian seasoning and cook for two minutes.

• Now add the rest of ingredients except yogurt and cilantro. Seal the pot with the lid and select "Manual" function for fifteen minutes.

• Use quick pressure release.

• Serve topped with yogurt and cilantro!

Instant Pot Chicken Recipes

6PTS Whole Chicken in an Instant Pot

Ready in 55 minutes,

6 servings

Freestyle Points value per serving: 6

Ingredients

- 1 whole chicken
- Any preferred seasonings
- 1 cup water
- 1 tablespoon coconut oil

Directions

1. Put a cup of water into the Instant Pot and add in the steam rack.
2. Heat the oil in a large skillet.
3. Coat the chicken with seasonings and then place in the oil and allow to brown for at least one minute on each side and then withdraw from heat.
4. Transfer the chicken to the Instant Pot on the steam rack.
5. Tight lid the Instant Pot and set to Chicken on high pressure. Adjust the time. Allow chicken to cook for not more than 30 minutes and the release steam naturally for 15 minutes. You can as well save the bones and make broth instead of throwing them.

Nutrition information

Calories: 339

Carbohydrates: 1g

Fats: 19g

Proteins: 38g

3PTS Pressure Cooked Chicken Romano

Ready in 25 minutes,

2 servings

Freestyle Points value per serving: 3

Ingredients:

- ½ cup all-purpose flour
- ½ teaspoon salt
- ½ teaspoon pepper
- 6 boneless skinless chicken
- 2 tablespoons oil
- 1 onion minced
- 1 10 ounce can tomato sauce
- 1 teaspoon vinegar
- 1 sliced mushrooms, fresh
- 1 tablespoon sugar
- 1 teaspoon garlic minced
- 1 tablespoon dried oregano
- 1 teaspoon dried basil

- 1 teaspoon of chicken bouillon granules
- 1 cup Romano cheese

Instructions

1. Sauté chicken in oil until golden brown. Add garlic and onion and cook until fragrant or become translucent.
2. Add the remaining ingredients with exception of Romano cheese. Stir well to combine. Secure the Instant Pot lid and set pressure valve to pressure.
3. Select the manual setting and set timer at 10-minutes. When the 10-minutes are up and, allow 10-minutes and then naturally release pressure.
4. Remove the lid, add Romano cheese and stir. Serve over pasta, rice.

Nutrition information

Calories: 108

Carbohydrates: 10g

Fats: 2g

Proteins: 10g

4PTS Delicious Shredded Chicken

Time: 25 mins

Number of servings: 4

Freestyle points per serving: 4

Ingredients:

- One pound skinless and boneless chicken breast
- One cup chunky salsa
- One tsp cumin
- Half tsp salt
- Pinch of oregano
- Black pepper for taste

Directions:

1. Season poultry on both sides with pepper, salt, cumin, and oregano.
2. Put seasoned chicken in your Instant Pot. Pour chunky salsa on the chicken.
3. Seal pot with lid and select "Poultry" function. Set timer for twenty-five minutes.
4. Use rapid pressure release method.
5. Transfer chicken to a platter and shred it with a couple of forks.
6. Serve and enjoy!

6PTS Freestyle Tasty Orange Chicken

Total Time: 20 mins

Number of servings: 4

Freestyle points per serving: 6

Ingredients:

- One pound skinless and boneless chicken breast, cut into cubes
- Two tbsp. flour
- Two tbsp. brown sugar
- One tbsp. ketchup
- One tbsp. coconut oil
- Half of cup chicken stock
- Three drops orange essential oil

Directions:

1. Put chicken and flour in one zip-lock bag and shake to coat meat well.
2. Add coconut oil in your Instant Pot and select "Sauté." Then add chicken in a pot and cook for two minutes. Then turn off a pot.
3. Now add chicken stock, ketchup, brown sugar, and orange essential oil in a pot and stir well.
4. Seal pot with lid, select "Manual" function to cook on high pressure for fifteen minutes. Then use rapid pressure release.
5. Serve with steamed rice and enjoy!
6.

6PTS Flex Whole Roasted Chicken

Total Time: 50 mins

Number of servings: 12

Freestyle points per serving: 6

Ingredients:

- Four-pound whole chicken
- One and a half cup chicken stock
- One tbsp. coconut oil
- One tsp paprika
- Half tsp salt
- Quarter tsp poultry seasoning
- Pinch of dried thyme
- Pepper for taste

Directions:

1. Add coconut oil in your Instant Pot and select "Saute" function. When oil heats up, put a chicken in the pot.
2. Mix paprika, salt, poultry seasoning, thyme, and pepper in a small bowl.
3. When the chicken becomes nice and brown on all sides, add that mix of seasoning and chicken stock.
4. Seal the pot with lid and select "Manual" function to cook on high pressure for twenty-five minutes.
5. Turn off the pot and allow pressure release naturally.
6. Serve and enjoy!

8PTS Chicken and Pancetta Risotto

Ready in 18-20 minutes, 4 servings,

Freestyle Points value per serving: 8

Ingredients:

- 1 large onion, chopped
- 2 garlic cloves, chopped
- 100g butter
- 1 tablespoon olive oil
- ½ tablespoon salt
- ½ tablespoon black pepper
- ½ tablespoon pancetta, diced
- 300g diced chicken
- 1 cup Arborio rice
- 4 tablespoon grated parmesan
- ½ cup white wine
- 2 cups chicken stock
- 1 tablespoon fresh thyme
- ½ tablespoon parmesan grated
- Black pepper, freshly ground
- 1 lemon grated zest
- Basil leaves

Directions:

1. Select 'fry' setting to preheat Instant Pot, and add the oil, and 30g of butter to the pan. Fry onions, garlic, pancetta and chicken for 2 minutes.
2. Stir in rice and season well, add thyme, and stir in the wine. Stop the pot. Pour in the stock and stir well.
3. Press the 'Manual' cooking button and adjust the cooking time to 12 minutes. Stir the risotto one last time and seal the pot with lid.
4. When the cooking time is over, stir the risotto to develop the creamy texture, and stir in the grated parmesan, and the remaining butter. Allow to for 3 minutes.
5. Top with extra parmesan, freshly ground black pepper basil leaves and grated lemon zest and serve.

Nutrition information

Calories: 582.7, Carbohydrates: 77.3g

Fats: 13.4g, Proteins: 35.1g

10PTS Pineapple Colada Chicken

Ready in 30 minutes,

4 servings

Freestyle Points value per serving: 10

Ingredients

- 2 pounds' chicken thighs, cut into one inch chunks

- 1 cup fresh pineapple chunks
- ½ cup full fat coconut cream
- 1 teaspoon cinnamon
- ¼ teaspoon salt
- 3 tablespoons coconut aminos
- ½ chopped green onion to garnish

Instructions

1. Place all ingredients, into Instant Pot, except green onions, and tightly close the lid.
2. Press Poultry setting button and the pot will set itself for 15 minutes, at high pressure.
3. Allow to cook and once cooking stops, turn off Instant Pot.
4. Allow natural release of pressure for 10 minutes and carefully open the lid and stir.
5. Stir in a teaspoon of arrowroot starch mixed with a tablespoon of water to thicken.
6. Sauté until sauce thickens to preference.
7. Turn off and serve with green onion garnish.

Nutrition information

Calories: 469

Carbohydrates: 37g

Fats: 25g

Proteins: 34g

5PTS Pressure Cooker Butter Chicken

Ready in 35 minutes,

5 servings

Freestyle Points value per serving: 5

Ingredients

- 3 lbs. boneless skinless chicken thighs, cut into pieces
- 1 tablespoon ghee
- 2 large onions, chopped
- 3 teaspoons salt
- 2 teaspoons garlic powder
- 2 tsp. ginger powder
- 2 teaspoons turmeric
- 2 teaspoons paprika
- 2 teaspoons cayenne powder
- 2 cups stewed tomatoes and the liquid
- 1 cup tomato paste
- 2 cans coconut milk
- 2 heaping tsp. garam masala
- ½ cup almond, sliced
- 1 cup cilantro

Instructions

1. Select the fry setting to melt ghee. Add 2 teaspoons of salt and onions and cook until onions are softened and translucent.
2. Add in garlic, ginger, paprika, turmeric and cayenne. Combine well and cook until fragrant.
3. Add in the canned tomatoes and the coconut milk, mix thoroughly with spices, add chicken and stir well to coat.
4. Cook the bite-sized chicken pieces of chicken for 8-10 minutes at high pressure. Stir in coconut cream, masala, tomato paste and most of the cilantro. Add salt if needed.
5. Top with the sliced almonds and use more cilantro to garnish.

3PTS One Pot Chicken

Ready in 20 minutes,

4 servings

Freestyle Points value per serving: 3

Ingredients

- 1 lb. chicken breasts, boneless skinless, frozen
- 1 cup water
- ½ cup flavorful liquid of choice

Instructions

1. Mix together the water and flavorful liquid. Place the frozen chicken in the Instant Pot l, and pour the mixture over the chicken. Tightly close the lid and valve
2. Select the 'Poultry' button and adjust the cooking time. For standard chicken breasts cook for 15 minutes or 30 minutes for extra-large breasts.
3. When cooking is done, open the pressure valve carefully and remove the lid and transfer the chicken breasts to a plate. Shred into bite-sized pieces. Turn on the Instant Pot's 'fry' mode to reduce the sauce. Return the shredded chicken back into the sauce and toss to coat.

Nutrition information

Calories: 125, Carbohydrates: 3g, Fats: 3g, Proteins: 22g

8PTS Chicken and Vegetable Noodle

Ready in 8-10 minutes,

2 servings

Freestyle Points value per serving: 8

Ingredients

Flavor Paste:

- ½ teaspoon sesame oil
- 2 tablespoons soy sauce
- 1 pinch of ground ginger
- ½ minced clove garlic
- ½ teaspoon sugar
- ½ cup lime juice
- 1 teaspoon chili sauce

Noodles:

- 50g dried rice noodles

- 2 small onions, sliced
- 3-4 sugar snaps, chopped into half
- ¼ red pepper, chopped
- 1 handful of kale
- 2 tablespoon cooked chicken, shredded
- ½ teaspoon corn flour
- 300ml boiling water, use kettle

Instructions

1. Mix all the ingredients to make flavor paste and put into a sealed jar until time of use.
2. Put all the noodle ingredients into a large mug, cover and refrigerate until time to eat.
3. Pour the flavor paste into the noodle cup and pour on the boiling water, stir well and cover. Leave for 3 minutes and stir again before serving.

Nutrition information

Calories: 384, Carbohydrates: 54g, Fats: 14.1g, Proteins: 9.6g

5PTS Instant Lemon Garlic Chicken

Ready in 30 minutes,

4 servings

Freestyle Points value per serving: 5

Ingredients

- 2 pounds' chicken breasts
- 1 teaspoon salt
- 1 diced onion
- 1 tablespoon avocado oil or ghee
- 4-5 minced garlic cloves
- 1 cup organic chicken broth
- 1 teaspoon dried parsley
- 1/2 teaspoon paprika
- 1/2cup white cooking wine
- 2 lemons
- 4 teaspoons arrowroot flour

Instructions

1. Set the Instant Pot onto the fry option and cooking fat   and add in onion
2. Allow the onions to cook until softened or for 5-10 minutes.
3. Add in the other remaining ingredients with exception of the arrowroot flour and tight lid the pot.
4. Choose the "Poultry" setting and ensure the steam valve is closed. Allow enough time to completely cook, release steam and then carefully remove lid
5. Thicken your sauce by making a slurry by removing some of the sauce from the pot.Add in the arrowroot flour, and reintroduce the slurry into the remaining liquid. Afterwards, stir and serve right.

Nutrition information

Calories: 205.3, Carbohydrates: 1.1g, Fats: 5.8g, Proteins: 35.1g

7PTS Barbecue Chili Chicken

Time: 25 mins

Number of servings: 4

Freestyle Points per serving: 7

Ingredients:

- One pound skinless and boneless chicken thighs
- One chopped onion
- Two tbsp. olive oil
- Two tbsp. Barbecue sauce
- Quarter cup water
- Quarter cup chili sauce
- One tbsp. vinegar
- Half tsp ground paprika
- Salt and ground black pepper to taste

Directions:

1. Pour olive oil in your Instant Pot and select "Sauté" function. When the oil heats up, add chicken and cook it for three minutes per side until it's browned.
2. Add paprika, salt, and ground in the pot. Then mix in a bowl onion, barbecue sauce, chili sauce, vinegar, and water. Pour that mixture over chicken.
3. Seal pot with lid and select "Manual" for fifteen minutes.
4. Release pressure with natural release method.
5. Serve hot and enjoy!

8PTS Cheesy Lemon Chicken

Time: 20 mins

Number of servings: 3

Freestyle points per serving: 8

Ingredients:

- Three boneless and skinless chicken breasts
- One cup spicy salsa
- Half cup crumbled feta cheese
- Quarter cup fresh lime juice
- One tbsp. olive oil
- Half tsp ground cumin
- Half tsp red chili powder

Directions:

1. Pour olive oil in your Instant Pot and select "Sauté" function.
2. Add chicken and cook it until becoming brown on both sides.
3. Remove meat from the pot. Then put salsa, lime juice, chili powder, and cumin in the pot and stir well.
4. Return chicken to the pot and select "Manual" function to cook on high pressure for eight minutes.
5. Use quick pressure release method and transfer chicken with sauce to a serving platter.
6. Sprinkle with crumbled cheese, serve, and enjoy!

10PTS Ultimate Flex Chicken Fajita Pasta

Total Time: 15 mins

Number of servings: 4

Freestyle points per serving: 10

Ingredients:

- One pound skinless and boneless cut into bite-sized pieces chicken breast
- Eight oz. dry penne pasta
- One can of tomatoes with juice
- One cup chicken broth
- Three tbsps. fajita seasoning
- Four minced garlic cloves
- One chopped onion
- Two seeded and diced bell peppers
- Two tbsps. olive oil

Directions:

• Pour olive oil in your Instant Pot and select "Saute" function. Put the chicken and a half of fajita seasoning when oil heats up.

• Stir well and continue to sauté until chicken becomes white.

• Add onion, bell pepper, garlic, and remaining fajitas seasoning. Mix well and sauté for two minutes.

• Now add chicken stock, pasta, and tomatoes with juice in a pot and stir again.

• Seal pot with lid and select "Manual" for six minutes. Then use rapid release method

• Serve and enjoy!

2PTS Veggie & Chicken broth

Ready in 45 minutes.

4 servings

Freestyle Points value per serving: 2

Ingredients

- 5 ribs celery
- 1 large onion
- 1 tablespoon apple cider vinegar
- 2 carrots
- 1 frozen or thawed chicken
- 4cloves garlic
- water
- 1tablespoon peppercorns
- 3 tablespoons salt water

Instructions

1. Combine all ingredients in the pressure cooker – cut the vegetables finely.
2. Add water to fill the pressure cooker
3. Cover cooker with lid and pressure gauge on your pressure cooker

4. Cook for 30 minutes while following pressure cooker instructions.
5. Allow cooker to depressurize on its own.
6. Open the cooker carefully and remove the chicken from the broth.
7. Strain the broth to remove veggies and peppercorns.
8. Use the broth for soup and serve.

Nutrition information

Calories: 77

Carbohydrates: 3.4g

Fats: 4.5g

Proteins: 6.6g

7PTS Turkey and Gluten Free Gravy

Ready in 1 hr. 15 minutes,

6 servings

Freestyle Points value per serving: 7

Ingredients

- 5-pound skin on, bone in bone-in turkey breast
- Salt
- black pepper
- 1-2 tablespoons ghee or butter
- 1 large onion, diced
- 2 carrots, diced
- 1 celery rib, diced
- 2 garlic cloves, well peeled and smashed
- 1-2 teaspoons dried sage
- ½ cup dry white wine
- 2 cups turkey or chicken bone broth
- 1 bay leaf
- ½ tablespoon tapioca starch

Instructions

1. Dry the turkey and season with salt and pepper. Heat cooking fat in pressure cooker over medium high heat. Fry if using an Instant Pot. Brown turkey breast for about 5 minutes, and then transfer to a plate, leave any fat in the pot.
2. Add in the chopped onion, celery and carrots, cook over medium heat until softened or about 5 minutes. Add and stir in garlic and sage, cook for 30 seconds until fragrant.
3. Add in the wine and cook for about 3 minutes and stir in the broth and bay leaf. Use a wooden spoon to scrape up any browned bits stuck at the bottom of the pot.
4. Place the turkey skin side up in the pot with accumulated juices.
5. Cover with lid and cook at high pressure for 35 minutes. Quick release pressure and remove the lid carefully.
6. Transfer the turkey to a carving board and tent loosely with foil, allow to rest as you prepare the gravy.
7. Carefully transfer the cooking liquid and vegetables preferably using an immersion blender to blender and puree until smooth. Cook at medium high heat until thickened and reduced. Adjust the seasoning to taste.

8. You can as well combine a tablespoon of tapioca starch with warm water and whisk into the gravy after cooking to make the gravy thicker.
9. Slice turkey and serve with hot gravy.

Nutrition information

Calories: 356.5, Carbohydrates: 8.4g, Fats: 24g, Proteins: 24.4g

8PFS Turkey Sage Burger

Cooking time: 15 minutes

Servings: 4

FS Points: 8

Ingredients

1½ pounds ground turkey

½ small onion, minced

1 teaspoon dried sage

1 egg

salt and pepper

2 tablespoons butter

4 burger buns

Instructions

1. Mix ground turkey, onion, dried sage, egg, salt and pepper in a bowl. Form the bowl content into four patties about ¼ inches thick.
2. Heat a large skillet and add butter.
3. Put patties onto the skillet and cook for about 6-7 minutes per side until well browned on the outside and no pink remains on the inside
4. Cut the buns in half and put patties inside.

Nutritional info

Calories: 377 , Fiber (g): 3.3 Sugar (g): 4.5 Protein (g): 31.8

5PFS Turkey Strips

Cooking time: 15 minutes

Servings: 4

Freestyle Points: 5

Ingredients

2 turkey breasts, cut into strips

¼ cup buttermilk

½ cup almond flour

1 tablespoon salt

1 garlic clove, minced

salt, pepper, to taste

½ teaspoon thyme

2 tablespoons olive oil

Instructions

1. Pour buttermilk into a bowl, add the turkey strips and marinate for 20 minutes.
2. Mix flour, salt, pepper and thyme. Heat oil in a skillet over medium heat.
3. Add garlic to the skillet and cook for 30 seconds.
4. Take the strips out of the bowl and dip each into the flour and seasoning mixture.
5. Put strips on a skillet and cook for 10 minutes and remove.

Nutritional info: Calories: 222, Saturated Fat (g): 1.9, Fiber (g): 1.1, Sugar (g): 4.5, Protein (g): 18.9

7PFS Frittata with Turkey Sausage

Cooking time: 10 minutes

Servings: 4

Freestyle Points: 7

Ingredients

2 tablespoons olive oil

½ lb ground turkey sausage

½ onion, chopped

2 cloves garlic, minced

2 cups small broccoli florets, steamed

2 oz. cream cheese

6 eggs

1 cup mozzarella, shredded

salt, pepper, to taste

Instructions

1. Heat olive oil in a pan and add turkey sausage, onions, and garlic.
2. Cook until the turkey is thoroughly browned, for 5-7 minutes. Season with salt and pepper.
3. Add broccoli, cream cheese, and six eggs.
4. Stir well and continue cooking over low heat until the mixture starts to firm up.
5. Sprinkle with mozzarella and transfer the pan content to the baking dish.
6. Preheat oven to 350 F. Bake for 3-4 more minutes until the eggs are firm and the cheese is browning.

Nutritional info

Calories: 242, Saturated Fat (g): 6.9, Fiber (g): 0.3, Sugar (g): 1.6, Protein (g): 19.2

8PFS Turkey Sausage Casserole

Cooking time: 30 minutes

Servings: 3

Freestyle Points: 8

Ingredients

1 tablespoon olive oil

8 oz Italian turkey sausage, sliced

1 onion, diced

8 ounces baby spinach, trimmed

1 cup fresh cremini mushrooms, sliced

2 tablespoons fresh basil, chopped

1/3 cup cheddar cheese, shredded

6 eggs

½ cup milk

¼ teaspoon of pepper

salt, to taste

Instructions

1. Heat the oven to 400 F. Grease a 9x13 inch baking dish with olive oil or cooking spray.
2. Heat olive oil in a large a skillet over medium heat. Sauté onions until translucent, for about 1-2 minutes.
3. Add sausages and cook for 8-10 minutes until cooked. Add spinach, mushrooms and basil. Season with salt and black pepper.
4. Sauté for 3-4 minutes or until the spinach is wilted. Remove from the heat.
5. Mix eggs and milk until fluffy with a beater or a whisk, for about 2-3 minutes.
6. Add egg mixture to the baking dish and top with sausage and spinach mixture. Sprinkle cheese on top.
7. Place casserole into the oven and bake for 15-20 minutes, until eggs are firm and cheese has melted.

Nutritional info

Calories: 336, Saturated Fat (g): 6.9, Fiber (g): 2.7, Sugar (g): 4.0

7PFS Potato Gratin Turkey Sausage

Cooking time: 1 hour

Serves: 4

Freestyle Points: 7

Ingredients

½ cup fat-free chicken broth, low-sodium

2 Italian turkey sausages

1 tablespoon butter

47

1 teaspoon olive oil

¾ cup Swiss cheese

3 cups onion, chopped

1 ½ pounds red potatoes, chopped

4 ounces cremini mushrooms

½ teaspoon kosher salt

2 tablespoons fresh thyme, chopped

cooking spray

Instructions

1. Preheat the oven to 400F.
2. Heat oil in a non-stick skillet over medium high heat. Put sausage into the skillet and sauté for about 5 minutes till brown, stir to crush. Take out sausage from the pan and drain.
3. Clean the pan. Melt butter on the pan, add onion and cook for 4 minutes stirring occasionally.
4. Add mushrooms, cook for 6 minutes and stir occasionally.
5. Add potatoes; sprinkle everything with salt and cook for another 5 minutes till brown stirring occasionally.
6. Add sausage and broth and take out from the heat.
7. Grease a ceramic baking dish with cooking spray. Put content of the pan to the dish and sprinkle with cheese.
8. Cover the dish with aluminum foil and bake for about 30 minutes. Remove the cover and cook another 15 minutes till golden.
9. Serve topped with thyme.

Nutritional info

Calories: 277, Saturated Fat (g): 5.7, Fiber (g): 4.4, Sugar (g): 5.7, Protein (g): 14

9PFS Beef Ragu with Tagliatelle

Cooking time: 50 minutes

Servings: 4

Freestyle Points: 9

Ingredients

9 oz Tagliatelle

14 oz extra lean minced beef

14 oz tomatoes, chopped

4 garlic cloves, chopped

2 carrots, finely diced

2 celery sticks, chopped

1 finely chopped onion

2 tablespoons tomato puree

1 teaspoon olive oil

½ teaspoon dried oregano

½ teaspoon sugar

1 bay leaf

2 cups water

salt and pepper, to taste

Instructions

1. Heat oil in a large non-stick frying pan, add minced beef and cook on a high heat for 5 minutes, stirring and breaking the meat up as it cooks.
2. Transfer cooked meat into a large saucepan, heat more olive oil in the frying pan and add carrots, onion and celery and cook over a low heat for 10 minutes, add a splash of water if required.
3. Stir in garlic and oregano and continue to cook for another 2 minutes, transfer the mixture into your saucepan.
4. Add sugar, bay leaf and water. Season with salt and pepper and bring to a boil, simmer for 45 minutes stirring occasionally until you have a rich and thick sauce.
5. Once your ragu is ready, cook pasta in accordance with the instructions on the packet and drain.
6. Divide into bowls and top with sauce.

Nutritional info

Calories: 363, Saturated Fat (g): 4, Fiber (g): 4.4, Sugar (g): 7.8, Protein (g): 25.7

8PFS Tomato Lime Beef Curry

Cooking time: 1 hour 30 minutes

Servings: 4

Freestyle Points: 8

Ingredients

1 lb ground beef (95% lean)

1 leck, thinly sliced

2 garlic cloves, minced

1 teaspoon fresh ginger

1 tablespoon red curry paste

1 ½ cups canned tomato sauce

1 teaspoon lime zest

1 tablespoon coconut aminos

½ cup canned light coconut milk

2 teaspoon lime juice

salt, to taste

Instructions

1. Heat oil in a skillet and brown beef for 5 minutes, transfer it to a saucepan.
2. Add leek, garlic, ginger, red curry paste, tomato sauce, lime zest, coconut aminos and salt to the saucepan.
3. Cook for 1 hour 5 minutes on high heat.
4. Add lime juice and coconut milk, stir and cook for another 15 minutes.

Nutritional info

Calories: 337, Saturated Fat (g): 9.4, Fiber (g): 2.6, Sugar (g): 5.9, Protein (g): 36.8

10PFS Delicious Beef Stew

Cooking time: 1 hour 30 minutes

Servings: 5

Freestyle Points: 10

Ingredients

1 ½ pounds lean beef, cut into cubes

1 ½ tablespoons almond flour

1 tablespoon black pepper

1 teaspoon five spice powder

4 cloves garlic, crushed and minced

1 tablespoon fresh lemongrass, chopped

2 tablespoons rice vinegar

½ tablespoon low sodium soy sauce

1 tablespoon honey

2 tablespoons olive oil

1 cup red onion, chopped

2 cups carrots, chopped

½ cup poblano pepper, diced

1 tablespoon jalapeno pepper, chopped

4 cups tomatoes, chopped

2 tablespoons tomato paste

2 cups acorn squash, cubed

3 cups low sodium beef broth

1 cinnamon stick

2 cardamom pods

2 anise star pods

Instructions

1. Mix almond flour, pepper and five spice powder in a bowl. Dip the meat into the flour mixture, coating generously.
2. Add garlic, lemongrass, rice vinegar, soy sauce, and honey. Mix well and refrigerate for at least 30 minutes.
3. Heat olive oil in a Dutch oven over medium heat. Add beef, onions and carrots. Sauté until meat is lightly browned, for about 3-5 minutes. Add poblano and jalapeno peppers, cook for another 1-2 minutes.
4. Add tomatoes, tomato paste, squash, beef stock, cinnamon stick, cardamom and anise star. Continue to cook, while stirring until well blended, for about 3-5 minutes.
5. Preheat the oven to 325°F.
6. Cover the Dutch oven and place into the oven to bake for 40 minutes, until meat is cooked through and tender.

Nutritional info

Calories: 460, Saturated Fat (g): 4.4

Fiber (g): 6

Sugar (g): 12.5

Protein (g): 48.4

6PFS Italian Beef Steak Rolls

Cooking time: 40 minutes

Servings: 4

Freestyle Points: 6

Ingredients

1 pound beef steak, thinly sliced

¼ cup low fat Italian salad dressing

1 cup red bell pepper, sliced

½ pound asparagus spears, trimmed

1 cup onion, sliced

1 teaspoon salt

1 teaspoon black pepper

cooking spray

Appliances

kitchen twine

Instructions

1. Put steaks into a bowl and sprinkle with Italian salad dressing, mix to coat. Set aside for 15 minutes.
2. Preheat the oven to 350°F and line a baking sheet with aluminum foil.
3. Remove the meat from the marinade and lay the slices out on a flat surface. Season with salt and black pepper.
4. Place red bell pepper, asparagus and onion pieces in the center of each piece of meat.
5. Roll up each slice of meat and secure with kitchen twine.
6. Heat the cooking spray in a skillet over medium high. Add steak rolls to the skillet and brown on all sides, for 1-2 minutes.
7. Transfer the steak rolls to the baking sheet. Place it into the oven and bake for 20 minutes, until the meat is cooked through and the vegetables are crisp tender.
8. Remove from the oven and let rest for 5 minutes before serving.

Nutritional info

Calories: 261

Saturated Fat (g): 2.7

Fiber (g): 2.4

Sugar (g): 3.8

Breakfast Recipes

Wake Up Sandwich

You will want to wake up to this early morning breakfast sandwich.

What to Use

1/4 cup liquid egg (whites OK too)

2 tbsp. Light shredded cheese

2 tbsp. Chopped green pepper

1 tbsp. sodium reduced ham

Pepper to taste

1/8 tsp Italian seasoning (optional)

1 whole-grain English muffin, toasted

What to Do

1. Find a bowl that is about the same size around as an English muffin and dishwasher safe.

2. In the bowl, mix together egg, cheese, pepper, ham, ground pepper and Italian seasoning (if using). Microwave on high for 1 minute. Turn the egg over and microwave for another 30 seconds to 1 minute.

3. Place egg on the toasted English muffin.

(Makes 1 Serving)

Calories per Serving: 247 Apple Oatmeal

A delicious and warming breakfast treat

What to Use

3 cups apple juice

1/2 tsp ground cinnamon

1 1/2 cups quick oats

1/2 cup chopped apple

1/4 cup maple syrup

1/4 cup raisins

1/4 cup chopped walnuts

4 tbsp. fat free vanilla yogurt

What to Do

1. Combine apple juice and cinnamon in a medium saucepan. Bring to a boil.

2. Stir in oats, chopped apple, maple syrup and raisins.

3. Reduce heat and cook until most of juice is absorbed, stirring occasionally. Fold in walnuts.

4. Top each bowl with a tablespoon of yogurt.

(Makes 4 Servings)

Calories per Serving: 271

Melon Smoothie

This smoothie harnesses the natural sweetness of the Watermelon.

What to Use

3 cups watermelon chunks

1 small banana, chopped

1 cup ice

1 1/2 cups 0% fat vanilla yogurt

What to Do

1. Put watermelon chunks, chopped banana, ice and yogurt in a blender. Blend until desired smoothness.

2. Pour into glasses.

(Serving Size 12 oz.)

Calories per Serving: 158

Whole Wheat Pancakes

A healthier choice than pre mixed pancake batters. Use wisely as that will add calories,

What to Use

1 cup whole wheat flour

1 tsp baking powder

1/2 tsp baking soda

1/8 tsp salt

1 egg, lightly beaten

1 cup low-fat buttermilk

2 tbsp. honey

What to Do

1. Whisk whole-wheat flour, baking powder, baking soda and salt in a medium bowl.

2, in a small bowl, combine egg, buttermilk and honey.

3. Make a well in dry what to Use and stir in egg and buttermilk mixture. Allow batter to rest for a few minutes.

4. set a nonstick frying pan to medium-high heat. Drop batter by 1/4 cupful's on to griddle or pan. Cook until the edges begin to dry and bubbles appear in the pancakes. Flip and cook for 1-2 minutes more.

(Makes 8 pancakes)

Calories per 2 Pancake Serving: 188

Morning Power Bar

Power up your morning workout with this healthy power bar.

What to Use

1 cup old-fashioned rolled oats

1/4 cup slivered almonds

1 tbsp. flaxseeds, preferably golden

1 tbsp. sesame seeds

1 cup unsweetened whole-grain puffed cereal

1/3 cup currants

1/3 cup chopped dried apricots

1/4 cup creamy almond butter

1/4 cup turbinated sugar

1/4 cup honey

1/2 teaspoon vanilla extract

1/8 teaspoon salt

What to Do

1. Preheat oven to 350°F. Coat an 8-inch-square pan with cooking spray.

2. Spread oats, almonds, flaxseeds and sesame seeds on a large, rimmed baking sheet. Bake until the oats are lightly toasted. Transfer to a large bowl. Add cereal, currants, apricots and raisins; toss to combine.

3. Combine almond butter, sugar, honey, vanilla and salt in a small saucepan. Heat over medium-low, stirring frequently, until the mixture bubbles.

4. Immediately pour the almond butter mixture over the dry what to Use and mix with a spoon or spatula until no dry spots remain.

5. Transfer to the prepared pan and press the mixture down firmly to make an even layer.

6. Refrigerate until firm, about 30 minutes

(Makes 8 Bars)

Calories per 1 Bar Serving: 244 calories

Texan Omelets Wrap

This wrap is a healthy taste of the south west.

What to Use

1 large egg

1 large egg white

1/2 teaspoon hot sauce, such as

Freshly ground pepper, to taste

1 tablespoon chopped scallions

1 tablespoon chopped fresh cilantro, or parsley (optional)

2 tablespoons prepared black bean dip

1 9-inch whole-wheat wrap, (see Ingredient note)

1 teaspoon canola oil

2 tablespoons grated pepper Jack or Cheddar cheese

1 tablespoon prepared green or red salsa, (optional)

What to Do

1. Set oven rack 6 inches from the heat source; preheat broiler.

2. Stir together eggs, hot sauce and pepper, scallions and cilantro (or parsley), if using.

3. If black bean dip is cold, warm it in the microwave on High for 10 to 20 seconds. Place wrap between paper towels and warm in the microwave on High for about 10 seconds. Spread bean dip over the wrap, leaving a 1-inch border all around.

4. Brush oil over a 10-inch nonstick skillet; heat over medium heat. Add the egg mixture and cook 20 to 30 seconds. Place the skillet under the broiler and broil just until the top is set, 20 to 30 seconds.

5. Slide the omelet onto the wrap. Sprinkle with cheese. Roll the wrap and serve with salad.

(Makes 1 Serving)

Calories per Serving: 321

Muesli

A classic breakfast that is power packed with dried fruit and healthy nuts.

What to Use

300g jumbo oats

100g All bran

25g wheat germ

100g dark raisins

140g ready-to-eat apricots, cut into chunks

50g golden linseeds

What to Do

1. Mix everything in a large bowl.

2. Store for up to 2 months, airtight.

3. Serve with Milk if you prefer

Calories per 1 Cup Serving: 124

Lunch Recipes

Pasta & Beans

This hearty dish combines filling beans with delicious pasta.

What to Use

1 1/2 tbsp. extra virgin olive oil

1 onion, chopped

2 tomatoes, chopped

1 (15 ounce) can beans

2 cups penne pasta

Salt to taste

What to Do

1. In a frying or sauté pan heat the oil. Add onion and then cook until translucent. Add tomatoes and beans. Let simmer for 10 mins.

2. Bring a large pot of lightly salted water to a boil. Add pasta. Cook until al dente then drain.

3. Mix pasta with bean mixture, toss to coat.

(Makes 4 Servings)

Calories per Serving: 286

Turkey Reuben

This healthy version of the Reuben sandwich still packs some great flavor.

What to Use

1/4 Cup Fat-free Thousand Island dressing

8 Slices Whole Wheat Bread

8 oz. Low Sodium Turkey Breast

1/2 Cup Sauerkraut (rinsed and drained)

4 Slices Reduced Fat Swiss cheese

Olive Oil Cooking Spray

What to Do

1. Spread dressing on one side of each slice of bread.

2. Stack sandwiches with turkey, sauerkraut and cheese.

3. Spray a large pan with olive oil spray and cook 2 sandwiches over medium heat for 4 minutes per side. Make sure bread is toasted and cheese is melted then serve hot.

(Makes 4 servings)

Calories per Serving: 268

The Healthy Roti

Experience the Caribbean with this West Indies inspired dish.

What to Use

1 tsp vegetable oil

1 small onion, peeled and sliced

1 cup chicken or vegetable broth

1 sweet potato, peeled and cubed

1 clove garlic, minced

1/2 tsp cumin

1/4 tsp each coriander, cinnamon and turmeric

1/2 tsp hot sauce

1 cup canned chickpeas

1/4 cup coconut milk

2-3 large roti or wheat flour tortillas

What to Do

1. Heat oil in a non-stick pan over medium heat. Add the onion; cook for 5 minutes. Stir in broth, sweet potato, garlic, cumin, coriander, cinnamon and turmeric.

2. Cover and cook, stirring every so often for 15 minutes or until potato is tender. Season with hot sauce.

3. Stir in chick-peas and coconut milk. Bring to a boil. Cook, stirring often, until chick-peas are heated through. Divide mixture between two roti shells. Roll to make a wrap.

(Makes 2 to 3 servings.)

Calories per Serving: 353

Sesame Noodles With Chicken

Harness the flavor of sesame in this Asian inspired dish.

What to Use

1 bag Japanese buckwheat soba noodles

5 tbsp. low-sodium soy sauce

2 tbsp. rice wine vinegar

1 tbsp. sesame oil

2 tbsp. honey

2 tsp honey mustard

1 tbsp. creamy peanut butter

3/4 lb. boneless, skinless chicken breast

5 scallions

What to Do

1. Cook noodles according to package.

2. In a large bowl whisk together next 6 What to Use to make dressing.

3. Cook chicken until cooked through. Shred and add to peanut mixture.

4. Add drained noodles, scallions and toss until combined.

(Makes 4 Servings)

Calories per Serving: 208

Mexican Lunch Minus The Meat

This tasty vegetarian dish is sure to please even the pickiest meat eater.

What to Use

1/2 small onion, chopped

1 can (15 1/2 ounces) crushed tomatoes

3/4 cup frozen corn kernels

1 can (3 1/2 ounces) chopped green chili peppers

1 can (14-19 ounces) black beans, rinsed and drained

1/2 cup instant rice

1 tsp ground cumin

What to Do

1. Heat a 2-quart pot coated with cooking spray over medium-high heat. Add the onion and cook, stirring, for 1 minute. Add tomatoes, corn, and chili peppers

2. Bring to a boil.

3. Add the beans, rice, and cumin. Remove from heat, cover, and let stand for 10 minutes.

(Makes 4 Servings)

Calories per Serving: 199

Healthy Lunch Pizza

This version of pizza packs all the flavor of take out, but a mere percentage of the calories.

What to Use:

1 toasted whole wheat pita

1/2 Cup chopped tomatoes

1/4 Cup shredded part-skim mozzarella

1/2 Cup grilled chicken breast

1/4 Cup chopped sun-dried tomatoes

Garlic and Oregano to taste

What to Do

1. Top 1 toasted whole wheat pita with tomatoes, mozzarella, grilled chicken breast, and chopped sun-dried tomatoes.

2. Sprinkle with minced garlic and oregano

3. Place under oven broiler until cheese bubbles.

Calories per Serving: 367.8

Grilled Veggies

This meal could be a dinner it is so filling. Quick enough for lunch though.

What to Use

1/3 cup balsamic vinegar

1 tbsp. Dijon mustard

3 garlic cloves, minced

1 tsp fresh rosemary, chopped

1/4 cup extra-virgin olive oil

1 red onion

2 zucchini

2 yellow squash

12 oz. asparagus, trimmed

1 roasted red bell pepper

1 1/2 cup lightly packed arugula, chopped

1 cup mixed baby greens

2 tbsp. fresh parsley, chopped

What to Do

1. In a medium bowl, whisk first 4 what to Use to make the dressing. Gradually add oil while stirring fast.

2. Heat barbecue or pan to medium high.

3. Brush onion, zucchini, yellow squash, and asparagus with 1/2 of the balsamic dressing. Grill or sauté vegetables until just cooked through, turning occasionally.

4. Allow veggies cool slightly, then cut into small pieces and place in large bowl.

Dinner Recipes

Tex-Mex Burger Wraps

These quick burger wraps will be a sure fire hit and they are much healthier than their fast food cousins.

What to Use

12 ounces lean ground beef

1 cup refried beans

1/2 cup chopped fresh cilantro

1 tbsp. chopped pickled jalapenos

1 avocado, peeled and pitted

1/2 cup prepared salsa

1/8 tsp garlic powder

4 whole-wheat tortillas

2 cups shredded romaine lettuce

1/2 cup shredded pepper Jack cheese

1 lime, cut into 4 wedges

What to Do

1. Preheat broiler. Coat a pan with light cooking spray.

2. Combine ground beef, beans, cilantro and jalapenos in a medium bowl.

3. Shape into four oblong patties and place on the prepared pan.

4. Broil the patties until done to your liking. Flip halfway through so both sides brow.

5. Mix avocado, salsa and garlic powder in a bowl.

6. Spread each tortilla with this mixture, then add lettuce and cheese.

7. Top each with a burger and roll into a wrap.

(Makes 4 Servings)

Calories per Serving: 394

Veggie Chili

This hearty chili will please even the carnivores in your house.

What to Use

1 small onion, chopped

1 large green bell pepper, chopped

3/4 cup chopped celery

3/4 cup dry red wine or water

3 cloves garlic, finely chopped

2 cans (14.5 ounces each) diced tomatoes, undrained

1 1/2 cups water

1/4 cup tomato paste

2 Vegetable Flavor Bouillon Cubes

1 tbsp. chopped fresh cilantro

1 tbsp. chili powder

1/2 tsp cumin

2 cans (15 ounces each) kidney beans, rinsed

What to Do

1. Cook onion, pepper, celery, wine and garlic in large saucepan over medium-high heat until vegetables are tender.

2. Add tomatoes with juice, water, tomato paste, bouillon, cilantro, chili powder and cumin; stir well.

3. Stir in beans. Bring to a boil; cover. Reduce heat to low; cook, stirring occasionally, for 45 minutes.

(Makes 6 Servings)Calories per Serving: 210

Lime Chicken

This Asian inspired dish is also full of vitamins from the citrus.

What to Use

Nonstick cooking spray

4 boneless, skinless chicken breast halves

3/4 cup Natural Apple Juice

Juice from **1** lime

2 tsp cornstarch

1 tsp Chicken Flavor Instant Bouillon

What to Do

1. Spray large, nonstick pan with nonstick cooking spray.

2. Cook chicken, turning once, for 8 to 10 minutes or until no longer pink in center. Remove from pan and keep warm.

3. Combine Apple Juice, lime juice, cornstarch and bouillon in small bowl.

4. Add to skillet; cook, stirring occasionally, until thick. Spoon sauce over chicken to serve.

(Makes 4 Servings)

Calories per Serving: 190

Mushroom and Scallion Chicken

Chicken is so versatile and boneless skinless chicken breast so healthy, that we had to bring you another tasty chicken recipe.

What to Use

1 tbsp. toasted sesame oil

1 small bunch scallions, sliced, whites and greens separated

1 small garlic clove, finely chopped

4 ounces shiitake mushrooms, stems removed and caps thinly sliced

4 cups water

1/4 cup low-sodium soy sauce

1 2-inch piece ginger, peeled and sliced

1 pound boneless, skinless chicken breasts, cut into 3/4 -inch cubes

What to Do

1. In a very large soup pot, heat the sesame oil over medium heat.

2. add the scallion whites and garlic; cook, stirring, about 1 minute. Add the mushrooms and cook until softened, about 3 minutes.

3. Pour the water into the pot. Add soy sauce and ginger. Let simmer for 2 minutes.

4. Place the chicken in the broth. Reduce heat to low; cover and poach until the chicken is just cooked through, about 7 minutes.

5. Transfer the chicken evenly to 4 bowls. Pour broth over the chicken. Garnish with the scallion greens.

(Makes 4 Servings)

Calories per Serving: 190

Broccoli And Shrimp

An Asian favorite, transformed in a quick and healthy dinner.

What to Use

2/3 cup chicken broth

1 tsp cornstarch

1 tbsp. minced garlic, divided

3 tsp extra-virgin olive oil, divided

1/4-1/2 tsp crushed red pepper

1 pound raw shrimp (21-25 per pound), peeled and deveined

1/4 tsp salt, divided

4 cups broccoli florets

2/3 cup water

2 tbsp. chopped fresh basil

1 tsp lemon juice

Freshly ground pepper to taste

Lemon wedges

What to Do

1. Combine chicken broth, cornstarch and half the garlic in a bowl; whisk until smooth.

2. Heat 1-1/2 tsp oil in a large nonstick pan over medium-high heat.

3. Add remaining garlic and crushed red pepper. Cook while stirring for about 30 seconds. Add shrimp. Sauté until shrimp are pink, about 3 minutes. Transfer to a bowl.

4. Add remaining oil to the pan. Add broccoli and a pinch of salt. Cook for 1 minute.

5. Add water, cover and cook until broccoli is crisp-tender, about 3 minutes. Transfer to the bowl with shrimp.

6. Add chicken stock mixture to the pan and cook, stirring, over medium-high heat, until thickened, 3-4 minutes.

7. Stir in basil and season with lemon juice and pepper. Add shrimp and broccoli; heat through. Serve with lemon wedges.

(Makes 4 Servings)

Calories per Serving: 178

Southwest Steaks w/Salsa Sauce

These steaks pack a punch of power, use your favorite cut of meat, but we love the rib-eye.

What to Use

2 4-ounce 1/2-inch-thick steaks, such as rib-eye, trimmed of fat

1 tsp chili powder

1/2 tsp kosher salt, divided

1 tsp extra-virgin olive oil

2 plum tomatoes, diced

2 tsp lime juice

1 tbsp. chopped fresh cilantro

What to Do

1. Rub both sides of steak with chili powder and 1/4 teaspoon salt.

2. Heat oil in a medium pan over medium-high heat. Add steaks and cook, turning once cook until it reaches your desired level of doneness. Cover steaks with foil and let rest while you make the salsa.

3. Add tomatoes, lime juice and remaining 1/4 teaspoon salt to the pan and cook, stirring often, until tomatoes soften, about 3 minutes.

4. Remove from heat, stir in cilantro and any accumulated juices from the steaks. Serve steaks topped with the salsa.

(Makes 2 Servings)

Grilled Eggplant & Portobello Sandwich

This vegetarian option is delicious and filling. It will be a crowd pleaser.

What to Use

1 small clove garlic, chopped

1/4 cup low-fat mayonnaise

1 tsp lemon juice

1 medium eggplant (about 1 pound), sliced into 1/2-inch rounds

2 large Portobello mushroom caps, gills removed

Canola or olive oil cooking spray

1/2 tsp salt

1/2 tsp freshly ground pepper

8 slices whole-wheat sandwich bread, lightly grilled or toasted

2 cups arugula, or spinach, stemmed and chopped if large

1 large tomato, sliced

What to Do

1. Preheat grill to medium-high.

2. Mash garlic into a paste on a cutting board with the back of a spoon. Combine with mayonnaise and lemon juice in a small bowl. Set aside.

3. Spray both sides of eggplant rounds and mushroom caps with cooking spray and season with salt and pepper. Grill the vegetables, turning once, until tender and browned on both sides. When cool enough to handle, slice the mushrooms.

4. Spread 1 1/2 teaspoons of the garlic mayonnaise on each piece of bread. Layer the eggplant, mushrooms, arugula (or spinach) and tomato slices onto 4 slices of bread and top with the remaining bread.

(Makes 4 Servings)

Calories per Serving: 209

Deserts Recipes

Fruity Parfaits

This treat uses non-fat yogurt for its creamy texture.

What to Use

2 8-ounce containers (2 cups) nonfat peach yogurt

1/2 pint fresh raspberries, (about 1 1/4 cups)

1 1/2 cups fresh, frozen or canned pineapple chunks

What to Do

1. Divide and layer yogurt, raspberries and pineapple into 4 glasses.

(Makes 4 Servings)

Calories per Serving: 109

Mocha Pudding

Homemade pudding is much healthier than store bough, and usually tastier too!

What to Use

1/4 cup sugar

3 tbsp. cornstarch

2 tsp instant coffee mix or espresso powder

1/2 tsp ground cinnamon

Pinch salt

2 cups low fat chocolate milk

2 ounces bittersweet chocolate, very finely chopped

1 tsp vanilla extract

What to Do

1. Whisk the sugar, cornstarch, coffee, cinnamon, and salt in a large saucepan. Whisk in milk over medium heat, then cook for about five minutes, stirring occasionally at first, then frequently at the end, until mixture thickens.

2. Remove from heat; add chocolate and vanilla, whisking until chocolate is smooth.

3. Serve warm or pour into five containers, placing plastic wrap directly on the pudding surface. Stays good in fridge for 5 days.

(Makes 5 Servings)

Calories per Serving: 194

Banana Quesadillas

This dessert take on a Mexican meal is a treat the whole family will enjoy.

What to Use

2 whole wheat tortillas

1 ripe banana

1 tbsp. peanut butter

A few chocolate chips (optional)

What to Do

Mash banana in bowl with potato masher.

2. Spread peanut butter and mashed banana on tortilla. Add chocolate chips, and top with other tortilla.

3. Warm in microwave for 20 seconds. (Time may vary depending on your microwave.)

4. Slice and serve.

(Makes 2 Servings)

Calories per Serving: 240 (without chocolate chips)

Broiled Mango

A quick and simple treat that will still impress guests.

What to Use

1 Peeled and Sliced Mango

Lime cut into wedges

What to Do

1. Position rack in upper third of oven and preheat broiler. Line a pan with foil.

2. Arrange mango slices in a single layer in the prepared pan. Broil until browned in spots, 8 to 10 minutes. Squeeze lime wedges over the broiled mango and serve.

(Makes 2 Servings)

Calories per Serving: 69

Sesame Squares

Sesame seeds are tasty calcium packed powerhouses.

What to Use

1/3 cup honey

1/3 cup peanut butter

3/4 cup nonfat dry milk

3/4 cup sesame seeds

1/4 cup raisins

1/4 cup shredded coconut

What to Do

1. In a large bowl, combine the honey, peanut butter, dry milk, sesame seeds, raisins, and coconut.

2. Spread the mixture into an 8 x 8-inch baking pan and refrigerate for 4 hours. Cut into 1-inch squares.

(Makes 32 Servings, 2 squares per serving)

Calories per Serving: 58.4

Easy Chocolate Cake

This recipe only takes one bowl, just imagine, easy chocolate cake!

What to Use

3/4 cup plus 2 tbsp. whole-wheat pastry flour

1/2 cup granulated sugar

1/3 cup unsweetened cocoa powder

1 tsp baking powder

1 tsp baking soda

1/4 tsp salt

1/2 cup nonfat buttermilk

1/2 cup packed light brown sugar

1 large egg, lightly beaten

2 tbsp. canola oil

1 tsp vanilla extract

1/2 cup hot strong black coffee

Confectioners' sugar, for dusting

What to Do

1. Preheat oven to 350°F. Coat a 9-inch round cake pan with cooking spray. Line the pan with a circle of wax paper.

2. Whisk flour, granulated sugar, cocoa, baking powder, baking soda and salt in a large bowl.

3. Add buttermilk, brown sugar, egg, oil and vanilla. Beat with an electric mixer on medium speed for 2 minutes. Add hot coffee and beat to blend. Pour the batter into the prepared pan.

4. Bake the cake until a skewer inserted in the center comes out clean, 30 to 35 minutes. Cool in the pan on a wire rack for 10 minutes; remove from the pan, peel off the wax paper and let cool completely. Dust the top with confectioners' sugar before slicing.

(Makes 12 Servings)

Calories per Serving: 139

Grapefruit Mango Sorbet

A super light dessert, that won't weigh you down on active nights.

What to Use

1/2 Cup water

1/4 Cup brown sugar

1/2 tsp ground ginger

2 lg grapefruit, cut into segments

4 sm scoops mango sorbet

Mint sprigs (optional)

What to Do

1. Simmer water, sugar, and ginger in small heavy saucepan until reduced to 1/4 cup, about 5 minutes.

2. Divide grapefruit sections among 4 dessert dishes. Pour spiced syrup over grapefruit, dividing evenly.

Top each portion with a scoop of mango sorbet and garnish with a mint sprig, if desired.

(Makes 4 Servings)

Calories per Serving: 226

Snack Recipes

G.O.R.P

The classic hiking accompaniment makes a great snack.

What to Use

1/2 ounce whole shelled (unpeeled) almonds

1/4 ounce unsalted dry-roasted peanuts

1/4 ounce dried cranberries

1 tbsp. chopped pitted dates

1 1/2 tsp chocolate chips

What to Do

1. Combine almonds, peanuts, cranberries, dates and chocolate chips in a small bowl.

(Makes 2 Servings)

Calories per Serving: 102

Sesame Carrots

A simple snack, but the sesame seeds add a nice touch

What to Use

2 cups baby carrots

1 tbsp. toasted sesame seeds

Pinch of dried thyme

Pinch of kosher salt

What to Do

1. Toss carrots with sesame seeds, thyme and kosher salt in a small bowl.

(Makes 3 Servings)

Calories per Serving: 33

Hummus

This fresh version of a store bought favorite will blow you away with its fresh taste

What to Use

2 cups canned garbanzo beans, drained

1/3 cup tahini

1/4 cup lemon juice

1 tsp salt

2 cloves garlic, halved

1 tbsp. olive oil

1 pinch paprika

1 tsp minced fresh parsley

What to Do

1. Place the garbanzo beans, tahini, lemon juice, salt and garlic in a blender or food processor. Blend until smooth. Transfer mixture to a serving bowl.

2. Drizzle olive oil over the garbanzo bean mixture. Sprinkle with paprika and parsley.

(Makes 8 Servings)

Calories per Serving: 77

Roasted Pumpkin Seeds

The Halloween favorite, is actually a nice healthy snack choice any time of year.

What to Use

1 1/2 cups raw whole pumpkin seeds

2 tsp butter, melted

1 pinch salt

What to Do

1. Preheat oven to 300 degrees F (150 degrees C).

2. Toss seeds in a bowl with the melted butter and salt. Spread the seeds in a single layer on a baking sheet and bake for about 45 minutes or until golden brown; stir occasionally.

(Makes 6 Servings)

Calories per Serving: 83

Cheesy Popcorn

This snack is so tasty you will think it can't be healthy.

What to Use

4 cups hot air-popped popcorn

1/2 cup freshly grated Parmesan cheese

Cayenne pepper, to taste

What to Do

1. Toss popcorn with Parmesan and cayenne to taste.

(Makes 4 Servings)

Calories per Serving: 75

Toasted Nuts

Nuts are full of heart healthy fats. A simple toasting will bring out their full flavor.

What to Use

1/2 cup chopped walnuts, or nut of your choice, you can also use a mix of nuts if you want.

What to Do

1. Preheat the oven to 350°F.

2. Spread the nuts out on a baking sheet.

3. Toast the nuts in the oven until they are lightly browned, about 8-10 minutes. Do NOT burn.

4. Cool and store in an airtight container for up to 2 weeks.

(Makes 8 Servings)

Calories per Serving: 40

Sun Dried Tomato Dip

This dip is perfect for veggies, tortillas or other healthy options like Melba toast.

What to Use

1 cup sun-dried tomatoes, rehydrated

1 tbsp. balsamic vinegar

1 cup non-fat cream cheese

1/2 cup non-fat sour cream

Basil leaves, for garnishing

What to Do

1. Puree the sun-dried tomatoes and balsamic vinegar in the food processor. Add the cream cheese and process until the mixture is smooth.

2. Add the sour cream and pulse until combined. (Be careful not to over process or the mixture will liquify.)

3. Transfer the spread to a serving bowl and garnish with fresh basil.

(Makes 10 Servings)

Calories per Serving: 52

We included extra recipes recommended with this program
These recipes are also easy to make so you don't have to worry about keeping up and maintaining your diet. Plus, the recipes are so delicious, you might even have a hard time tearing yourself away from the kitchen! Enjoy

Soup Recipes
BEEF LOADED SOUP

What to Use:
- 3 cups of beef broth (fat-free)
- 10 ounces of Rotel diced tomatoes and green chilies – undrained
- 2 cloves of garlic – diced
- 2 tablespoons of tomato paste

- ½ medium yellow onion – diced
- 2 cups of chopped cabbage
- 1 cup of carrots – shredded
- 1 cup of fresh mushrooms – sliced
- 15 ounces of green beans – drained
- 15 ounces of pinto beans – drained then washed
- 1 medium yellow squash – diced
- 1 medium zucchini – diced
- 1 teaspoon of dried oregano
- 1 teaspoon of dried basil
- Pepper
- Salt

What to Do:

- Prepare a large stock pot and grease the bottom with cooking spray. Add the onions, carrots, and garlic and cook until the vegetables are tender.
- Except for the zucchini, add all them to Use into the pot and stir. Simmer for 10 minutes.
- Throw in the zucchini and simmer again for 10 minutes.

Nutrition Facts:

- Calories – 200
- Total Fat – 0.73g
- Total Carbohydrate – 36.6g
- Protein – 12.5g
- Calcium – 96mg
- Iron – 3.35mg
- Potassium – 937mg
- Sodium – 383mg
- Zinc – 1.3mg
- Thiamin – 0.39mg

- Riboflavin – 0.21mg
- Niacin – 2.14mg

CHICKEN STEW

What to Use:

For the sofrito

- ½ tablespoon of olive oil
- 4 cloves of garlic – finely chopped
- 6 scallions – chopped
- 2 tomatoes – diced
- 1 teaspoon of ground cumin
- 1/3 cup of diced red bell pepper
- 1 teaspoon of annatto seed powder
- 1 ½ teaspoons of salt
- For the stew
- 8 large chicken drumsticks – skin removed
- 6 ounces of light beer
- ½ teaspoon of garlic powder
- 1 cup of water
- ½ cup of cilantro – chopped
- Salt

What to Do:

- Prepare a deep pan and heat the olive oil. Add the garlic and scallions and cook for 2 minutes. Add the bell pepper and tomatoes. Stir and season with annatto, cumin, and salt. Set aside.

- Season the drumsticks with garlic and salt. Place the chicken on the same pan and cook until both sides are slightly browned. Replace the cooked vegetables into the pan and add in the cilantro, water, and beer. Season with salt as needed. Place a lid on the pan and simmer for 30 minutes on low heat.

- Serve over warm rice. Enjoy!

Nutrition Facts:

- Calories – 110

- Fat – 3g
- Protein – 14g
- Carbohydrates – 5g
- Fiber – 1g
- Sugar – 1g
- Cholesterol – 48mg
- Sodium – 382mg

CHICKEN NOODLE SOUP

What to Use:

- 1lb of chicken breasts (skinless and boneless)
- 8 cups of chicken broth (fat-free)
- 1 teaspoon of olive oil
- 3 large carrots – chopped
- 1 small yellow onion – chopped finely
- 3 stalks of celery – chopped
- 1 teaspoon of dried thyme
- 2 cloves of garlic – minced
- 1 teaspoon of dried dill
- ½ teaspoon of dried rosemary
- Juice from ½ lemon
- 4 ounces of egg noodles
- Pepper
- Salt
- ¼ cup of fresh parsley – chopped

What to Do:

- Add all ingredients to Use in a slow cooker except for the parsley, lemon juice and egg noodles.
- Cook for 8 hours on low settings. Remove the chicken from the slow cooker and chop into smaller pieces. Set aside.

- Add the parsley, lemon juice, and egg noodles into the slow cooker and cook for 15 minutes. Return the chicken into the slow cooker and stir.
- Serve while still hot.

Nutrition Facts:

- •Calories – 160
- •Fat – 3g
- •Protein – 16g
- •Carbohydrates – 15g
- •Fiber – 2g

COCONUT CHICKEN STEW

What to Use:

- •15 ounces of light coconut milk
- •2 cloves of garlic – minced
- •8 ounces of chicken breasts (skinless and boneless)
- •2 tablespoons of fresh ginger – grated
- •1 head of bok choy – chopped
- •1 small onion – halved then thinly sliced
- •5 cups of chicken broth (fat-free)
- •3 small pieces of lemongrass stalks
- •2 teaspoon of sugar
- •2 serrano peppers – diced
- •3 tablespoons of fish sauce
- •1/3 cup of fresh cilantro – chopped
- •Juice from 4 limes

What to Do:

- Prepare a Dutch oven and set over medium-high heat. Slightly grease with olive oil.
- Mash the lemongrass stalks using the flat side of a kitchen knife to release its flavor. Add the garlic, onion, lemongrass, ginger, serrano peppers, and ¼ cup of chicken broth in the Dutch oven. Stir and cook for 5 minutes.

- Add in the meat together with the remaining chicken broth. Bring to boil then lower heat to medium. Cover the Dutch oven with a lid and simmer until the chicken is thoroughly cooked.
- Remove the chicken from the Dutch oven and transfer on a dish. Shred the meat using two forks then replace it into the Dutch oven.
- Stir in the sugar, lime juice, fish sauce, bok choy, cilantro, and coconut milk. Cook until the bok choy becomes tender. Remove the lemongrass stalks and serve.

Nutrition Facts:
- Calories – 125
- Fat – 4g
- Carbohydrates – 9g
- Protein – 12g
- Fiber – 1.5g

CLASSIC TOMATO SOUP

What to Use:
- 2lbs of fresh tomatoes – chopped
- 1 tablespoon of light butter
- 1 medium yellow onion – chopped
- 1 ½ cups of chicken broth (fat-free)
- ½ cup of grated parmesan cheese
- 2 bay leaves
- Pepper
- Salt
- 1 cup of 2% milk

What to Do:
- Prepare a large saucepan and set over medium-high heat. Melt the butter in the saucepan then add in the onion. Cook until the onion starts to soften.

- Stir in the fresh tomatoes and ½ cup of chicken broth. Cook until the tomatoes begin to break apart and release its juices.
- Throw in the bay leaves into the saucepan and pour in the remaining chicken broth. Adjust heat to low and cover the saucepan with a lid. Simmer for 10 minutes.
- Add in the milk and cheese and stir continuously. Cook for 3 minutes to melt the cheese.
- Remove the saucepan from the heat and discard the bay leaves. Pour the soup into a blender and puree until the soup becomes smooth and creamy. Ladle into bowls and serve while still hot.

Nutrition Facts:

- Calories – 160
- Fat – 6g
- Carbohydrates – 15g
- Protein – 10g
- Fiber – 3g

SWEET POTATO SOUP

What to Use:

- 6 sweet potatoes – peeled then diced
- 1 cup of chicken broth (fat-free)
- 1 cup of 2% milk
- 1 teaspoon of orange zest
- Ground chipotle powder
- Pepper
- Salt

What to Do:

- Turn on oven and set to 425F. Prepare a baking sheet and line with parchment paper. Lightly grease with cooking spray.
- Arrange the diced sweet potatoes on the baking sheet and spray cooking spray on top. Season with pepper and salt.

- Place in the oven and roast for 30 minutes. The potatoes should be tender by then.
- Add the potatoes, orange zest, milk, and chicken broth in a blender and puree until the mixture becomes smooth.
- Pour into a small saucepan and reheat. Taste and adjust seasoning as necessary. Sprinkle chipotle powder on top before serving.

Nutrition Facts:

- Calories – 132
- Fat – 1g
- Carbohydrates – 28g
- Protein – 3.5g
- Fiber – 4g

FRENCH ONION SOUP

What to Use:

- 2 large sweet onions – sliced
- 4 cloves of garlic – minced
- 2 large red onions – sliced
- 1 teaspoon of chopped fresh thyme
- 1 tablespoon of Worcestershire sauce
- 1 tablespoon of balsamic vinegar
- 1 teaspoon of salt
- ½ cup of red wine
- 1 bay leaf
- ½ teaspoon of freshly ground pepper
- ¼ cup of minced fresh chives
- 42 ounces of beef broth (fat-free)
- 1 cup of shredded fontina cheese
- 6 slices of whole wheat bread

What to Do:

- Prepare a large saucepan and set over medium-high heat. Spray with cooking spray. Add the red onions and sweet onions and toss. Cover the pan with a lid and reduce the heat to medium. Cook for 8 minutes.
- Add the bay leaf, garlic, and thyme and cook for 4 minutes. Leave the saucepan uncovered and stir often while cooking.
- Stir in the balsamic vinegar, red wine, salt, Worcestershire sauce, and pepper. Return the heat to medium-high then simmer. Cook for 2 minutes and stir often.
- Stir in the beef broth then bring to boil. Once boiling, reduce the heat to medium and cook for 3 minutes.
- Remove the saucepan from the heat and stir in the chives.
- Toast the whole wheat bread slices.
- Sprinkle the cheese on top of the soup and serve with the toasted bread.

Nutrition Facts:
- •Calories – 138
- •Fat – 6g
- •Carbohydrates – 18g
- •Protein – 15g
- •Fiber – 4g

CRAB BISQUE

What to Use:
- •16 ounces of lump crabmeat
- •2 cups of milk (fat-free)
- •2 cups of chicken broth (fat-free)
- •1 cup of dry sherry
- •1 cup of fresh corn kernels
- •1 ½ cups of cauliflower – cut into small pieces

- 1 cup of diced yellow bell pepper
- 1 cup of chopped onion
- 1 large celery stalk – cut into small pieces
- 1 ½ cups of diced red bell peppers
- 2 tablespoons of sour cream (fat-free)
- 1 tablespoon of light butter
- 2 bay leaves
- 1 teaspoon of smoked paprika
- 1 teaspoon of salt
- 1 teaspoon of thyme
- ¼ teaspoon of black pepper

What to Do:

- Prepare a large saucepan and set over medium heat.
- Melt the butter then add in the onion, corn, bell peppers, and celery. Cook for 5 minutes while stirring often. Add paprika and cauliflower and cook for another 2 minutes. Stir often.
- Add sherry and cook for 5 minutes. Scrape browned bits from the bottom of the pan. Add the chicken broth and bring to boil.
- Reduce heat and cook for 15 minutes while stirring occasionally. The cauliflower should be tender at this point. Discard the bay leaves.
- Working in two batches, pour the vegetable mixture into a food processor and puree until smooth. Return the puree into the saucepan and stir in the sour cream, milk, bay leaves, crab, salt, pepper, and thyme.
- Cook for 5 minutes and stir occasionally. Once heated, pour into serving bowls and top with fresh parsley. Enjoy!

Nutrition Facts:

- Calories – 158
- Fat – 3g
- Carbohydrates – 12g

- Protein – 19g
- Fiber – 4g

Taco Chicken Chili

What to Use:

- 1 onion – chopped
- 16 ounces of kidney beans – rinsed then drained
- 16 ounces of black beans – rinsed then drained
- 8 ounces of tomato sauce
- 30 ounces of diced tomatoes with chilies
- 10 ounces of frozen yellow corn
- 1 tablespoon of chili powder
- 1 packet of taco seasoning (reduced sodium)
- ¼ cup of fresh cilantro
- 24 ounces of chicken breasts (boneless and skinless)

What to Do:

- Mix together the onion, kidney beans, black beans, tomato sauce, diced tomatoes, yellow corn, chili powder, and taco seasoning in a slow cooker.
- Place the chicken breasts on top of the mixture and press the meat down slightly.
- Cook for 10 hours on low settings.
- Remove the chicken breasts and use two forks to shred the meat. Return the shredded meat into the slow cooker and stir.
- Transfer in a serving dish and top with cilantro before serving. Enjoy!

Nutrition Facts:

- Calories – 219
- Fat – 3g
- Carbohydrates – 26g
- Fiber – 7g
- Protein – 22g

- Sugars – 10g
- Sodium – 810mg

BLACK BEAN SOUP

What to Use:

For the beans

- 1lb of dry black beans
- 1 small onion – quartered
- 1 small red bell pepper
- 3 bay leaves
- 2 cloves of garlic

For the soup

- 1 tablespoon of olive oil
- ½ cup of chopped parsley
- 1 large onion – minced
- 1 red pepper – minced
- 5 cloves of garlic – minced
- 2 medium carrots – shredded
- ¼ cup of white wine
- 1 tablespoon of red wine vinegar
- 1 teaspoon of oregano
- 1 teaspoon of cumin
- Black pepper
- Salt
- 1 chicken bullion

What to Do:

- Prepare a large pot with 8 cups of water. Rinse the black beans and add into the pot. Cover the pot with a lid and bring the water to boil. Once boiling, remove pot from the heat and let sit for 1 hour. Do not remove the lid.
- Drain the water from the pot and replace with 10 cups of cold water.

- Add the small onion, bell pepper, bay leaves, and 2 cloves of garlic into the pot of beans. Bring to boil then lower the heat and simmer for 1 hour. Stir occasionally.
- Prepare a frying pan and set over low heat. Add the olive oil.
- Once the oil is hot, add in the onion, carrots, red pepper, parsley, and remaining garlic. Season with pepper and salt and cook for 5 minutes. Stir occasionally.
- Add the cooked vegetables into the pot after simmering the beans for an hour.
- Add the vinegar, wine, oregano, cumin, salt, pepper, and bullion. Add more water if necessary.
- Cover the pot with a lid and simmer for 20 minutes.
- Once done, remove the bay leaves and puree half of the mixture using an immersion blender to thicken the soup. Taste and add more seasonings as necessary. Serve while still hot. Enjoy!

Nutrition Facts:

- Calories – 234.4
- Fat – 2.6g
- Protein – 13.6g
- Carbohydrates – 40.1g
- Fiber – 19.6g

CLASSIC CORN SOUP

What to Use:

- ½ teaspoon of olive oil
- 1 clove of garlic – chopped
- 1/3 cup of chopped scallions
- 3 ½ cups of fresh corn kernels
- 5 cups of 1% milk
- 1 russet potato, peeled then diced

- 2 tablespoons of chopped fresh cilantro
- 1 chicken bullion
- Fresh pepper
- Salt
- ¼ cup of sour cream (reduced fat)
- 6 tablespoons of crumbled queso fresco

What to Do:

- Prepare a Dutch oven and set over medium heat.
- Heat the olive oil then add in the garlic and scallions. Cook for a minute while stirring continuously.
- Add the potato, corn, 1 tablespoon of fresh cilantro, milk, and bullion into the Dutch oven. Stir and bring the mixture to a boil.
- Lower heat to a simmer then cover with a lid. Cook for 35 minutes. Stir occasionally.
- Remove the Dutch oven from heat and stir in the sour cream. Puree the mixture in an immersion blender.
- Return the soup in the Dutch oven and set over low heat. Taste and adjust seasoning according to preference.
- Pour into a serving bowl and top with the remaining cilantro. Serve while still hot. Enjoy!

Nutrition Facts:

- Calories – 257
- Fat – 8g
- Carbohydrates – 36g
- Fiber – 3g
- Protein – 14g
- Sugar – 14g
- Sodium – 474mg
- Cholesterol – 22mg

MAIN DISH RECIPES

Insane Burger

What to Use:

- 1 small hamburger bun
- 1 slice of cheddar cheese (fat-free)
- 1 vegan burger
- 1 pineapple ring – packed in juice
- 1 lettuce leaf
- 1 slice of tomato
- 1 teaspoon of mayonnaise (fat-free)
- 1 tablespoon of thick teriyaki marinade

What to Do:

- Prepare a grill pan and set over medium-high heat. Grease with cooking spray and place the pineapple ring on top. Grill each side for 3 minutes. Set aside until needed.
- Microwave the burger for 1 minute then transfer on a microwave-safe plate. Pour ½ of the teriyaki marinade on the burger and spread to evenly coat both sides. Place the cheese on top of the burger and microwave for another 30 seconds.
- Place the burger on the bottom half of the burger bun and pour the remaining teriyaki marinade on top. Add the pineapple, tomato, and lettuce and spread the mayonnaise under the top half of the burger bun. Assemble and consume immediately. Enjoy!

Nutrition Facts:

- Calories – 305.5
- Cholesterol – 2.8mg
- Sodium – 1642.4mg
- Carbohydrates – 46.7g
- Protein 24.5g

BARBACOA BEEF

What to Use:

- 3lbs of beef eye of round bottom roast – trim fat
- ½ medium onion

- 5 cloves of garlic
- Juice of ½ lime
- 1 tablespoon of ground cumin
- 4 chipotles in adobo sauce
- ½ teaspoon of ground cloves
- 1 tablespoon of ground oregano
- 3 bay leaves
- Pepper
- Salt
- 1 cup of water
- 1 teaspoon of oil

What to Do:

- Add the onion, garlic, cumin, lime juice, chipotles, oregano, and cloves in a blender. Puree the spices then set aside until needed.
- Cut the beef into 4-inch chunks and season with pepper and salt. Prepare a skillet and set over high heat. Add the oil and brown the beef chunks. Once done, transfer the meat in a pressure cooker and add the bay leaves, water, and pureed spices. Stir then simmer for 2 hours on low settings.
- Discard the bay leaves. Remove the beef chunks from the pressure cooker and place on a dish. Shred the meat using two forks. Return the meat into the pressure cooker and taste. Adjust seasonings if necessary.
- Simmer uncovered for another 10 minutes. Serve and enjoy!

CHICKEN SALAD

What to Use:

- 2 ½ cups of chopped cooked chicken
- 1 cup of chopped apple
- 3 stalks of celery – chopped
- ¼ cup of dried cranberries

- •2 tablespoons of light mayonnaise
- •½ cup of plain Greek yogurt (non-fat)
- •2 tablespoons of chopped parsley
- •2 teaspoons of lemon juice
- •Pepper
- •Salt

What to Do:

- In a salad bowl, combine the celery, chicken, cranberries, and apple.
- Combine the mayonnaise, lemon juice, and yogurt in a separate bowl. Add in the parsley and stir.
- Add the dressing into the salad bowl and mix well. Use pepper and salt to season according to your preference. Serve and enjoy!

Nutrition Facts:

- •Calories – 220
- •Fat – 5g
- •Carbohydrates – 13g
- •Fiber – 2g
- •Protein – 28g

PITA BREAD PIZZA

What to Use:

- 1 8-inch pita bread
- 2 tablespoons of mozzarella cheese (low-fat)
- 2 tablespoons of Alfredo sauce
- 1 teaspoon of olive oil
- ½ cup of fresh baby spinach
- 1 cup of fresh mushrooms
- Parmesan cheese
- Garlic salt

What to Do:

- Turn on oven and set to 425F.

- Prepare a small saucepan and set over medium-high heat. Heat the olive oil and cook the mushrooms for 5 minutes. Remove the mushrooms from the heat then set aside.
- Place the pita bread on a small baking pan. Spread the sauce on top of the bread. Top with mozzarella cheese, spinach, mushrooms, parmesan cheese, and garlic salt.
- Place the baking pan in the oven and bake for 10 minutes. Slice and serve. Enjoy!

CHICKEN ENCHILADAS

What to Use:

- 4 chicken breasts (boneless and skinless)
- 1 packet of taco seasoning (reduced sodium)
- 16 ounces of salsa
- ½ teaspoon of garlic powder
- 8 whole wheat tortillas
- Pepper
- Salt
- 1 cup of cheddar cheese (reduced fat) – shredded
- 10 ounces of enchilada sauce

What to Do:

- Grease the slow cooker with cooking spray. Place the chicken breasts at the bottom of the slow cooker. Add in the taco seasoning, salsa, pepper, salt, and garlic powder.
- Cook for 6 hours on low settings.
- Once done, remove the chicken breasts from the slow cooker and use two forks to shred the meat.
- Return the shredded meat into the slow cooker and stir.
  - Turn on oven and set to 350F.

- Place ¾ cup of the chicken mixture inside a tortilla and roll up. Repeat the same procedure until all the tortillas and chicken mixture are used up.
- Prepare a baking pan and lightly grease with cooking spray. Place the rolled up tortilla in the baking pan. Pour the enchilada sauce over the tortillas and sprinkle cheddar cheese on top. Bake for 25 minutes.

Nutrition Facts:
- •Calories – 138
- •Fat – 2.48g
- •Carbohydrates – 19.4g
- •Protein – 9.6g
- •Cholesterol – 11.93mg

GARLIC TUNA BURGER

What to Use:
- •12 ounces of canned tuna fish – drained then flaked
- •2 scallions – chopped finely
- •½ cup of plain panko bread crumbs
- •¼ cup of fresh parsley – chopped finely
- •Juice of 1 lemon
- •2 cloves of garlic – minced
- •1 large egg
- •3 tablespoons of sour cream
- •¼ teaspoon of pepper
- •¼ teaspoon of salt

What to Do:

- Turn on oven and set to 400F. Prepare a baking sheet and line with parchment paper.
- In a mixing bowl, combine the bread crumbs, tuna, parsley, scallions, lemon juice, garlic, egg, sour cream, pepper, and salt. Using your hands, form 4 patties from the tuna mixture and place on the baking sheet. Bake in the oven for 20 minutes.
- Serve with toasted bread, lettuce, and fresh slices of tomatoes. Enjoy!

Nutrition Facts:

- •Calories – 175
- •Fat – 4g
- •Carbohydrates – 10g
- •Fiber – 0g
- •Sugars – 0g
- •Protein – 24g

CHEESY TACO PASTA

What to Use:

- •8 ounces of wheat pasta
- •1 packet of taco seasoning (reduced sodium)
- •1lb of 95% lean ground beef
- •1 ½ cups of chunky salsa
- •¼ cup of sour cream (fat-free)
- •½ cup of water
- •¾ cup of shredded extra-sharp cheddar cheese
- •¾ cup of shredded 2% cheddar cheese (reduced fat)
- •Pepper
- •Salt

What to Do:

- Prepare the wheat pasta according to package
- Prepare a pan and set over medium-high heat. Add the ground beef and break it up while it cooks. Once done, remove the excess grease.
- Add the salsa, taco seasoning, and water. Lower the heat and simmer for 5 minutes.
- Once the pasta is cooked, drain and add into the pan with the beef mixture. Add the cheese, pepper, salt, and sour cream. Stir and mix thoroughly. Once the cheese has melted, remove the pan from the heat and transfer into a serving dish. Serve immediately. Enjoy!

Nutrition Facts:

- Calories – 376
- Carbohydrates – 37g
- Sugars – 5g
- Fat – 13g
- Protein – 29g
- Fiber – 6g

Salad and Side Dish Recipes
COBB SALAD

What to Use:

For the salad

- 2 cups of shredded romaine lettuce
- 2 large hard-boiled eggs – whites and yolks separated then cut small
- ½ head of Boston lettuce – chopped coarsely
- 5 slices of bacon – cooked then crumbled
- 6 ounces of chicken breasts – cooked then diced
- 1 Hass avocado – cut into ½-inch pieces
- ½ cup of crumbled blue cheese (reduced fat)
- 2 tomatoes – finely chopped

For the vinaigrette

- •1 medium ripe tomato
- •1 tablespoon of red wine vinegar
- •1 clove of garlic – crushed
- •3 tablespoons of extra-virgin olive oil
- •1 tablespoon of lemon juice
- •1 teaspoon of Dijon mustard
- •½ teaspoon of oregano
- •2 tablespoons of water
- •1 tablespoon of minced shallot
- •Pepper
- •Salt

What to Do:

- To make the salad, arrange the lettuce leaves at the bottom of a large salad platter. Then, arrange the bacon, chicken, egg, tomato, and avocado in rows on top of the greens.
- To make the vinaigrette, add the tomato in a food processor and chop. Add in the vinegar, garlic, water, lemon juice, oregano, Dijon mustard, pepper, salt, and oregano. Pulse until the mixture becomes smooth. Add in the shallot and mix until properly combined. Set aside for a few minutes to let the flavors combine.
- Pour the vinaigrette on top of the salad and serve. Enjoy!

Nutrition Facts:

- •Calories – 141.9
- •Fat – 9.3g
- •Carbohydrates – 5.2g
- •Fiber – 3g
- •Sugar – 0.3g
- •Protein – 11g

FIESTA SALAD

What to Use:

- •2 cloves of garlic – minced
- •1 tablespoon of extra-virgin olive oil
- •3 tablespoons of fresh lime juice
- •1 teaspoon of cumin
- •½ teaspoon of salt
- •Crushed red pepper flakes
- •1 cup of canned chickpeas – rinsed then drained
- •15 ounces of black beans – rinsed then drained
- •¼ cup of minced red onion – diced finely
- •1 cup of cherry tomatoes – halved
- •1 medium avocado – diced
- •¼ cup of cilantro – chopped

What to Do:

- Whisk together the lime juice, garlic, cumin, oil, salt, and crushed red pepper flakes in a large bowl.
- Add the chickpeas, black beans, onion, tomato, and cilantro. Gently mix in the avocado once ready to serve. Enjoy!

Nutrition Facts:

- •Calories – 335
- •Fat – 11.5g
- •Carbohydrates – 47g
- •Fiber – 15.5g
- •Protein – 14g
- •Sugar – 0.4g
- •Sodium – 481.6mg
- •Cholesterol – 0mg

WINTER SALAD

What to Use:

- •1lb of chicken breasts (skinless and boneless) – cooked then cut into strips
- •2 cups of red cabbage – shredded

- •5 cups of romaine lettuce – chopped
- •1 small red onion – sliced thinly
- •2 persimmons – peeled and seeded then diced
- •1 pear – cored then diced
- •1/3 cup of pine nuts – toasted
- •½ cup of pomegranate
- •1/3 cup of red wine vinegar
- •2 tablespoons of walnut oil
- •Pepper
- •Salt
- •1 tablespoon of honey

What to Do:

- Combine the chicken, cabbage, lettuce, onion, persimmons, pear, pine nuts, and pomegranate in a salad bowl.
- Whisk together the vinegar, walnut oil, and honey. Drizzle mixture over the salad and toss until well-coated. Season with pepper and salt as desired.
- Serve and enjoy!

Nutrition Facts:

- •Calories – 238
- •Fat – 10.5g
- •Carbohydrates – 15g
- •Protein – 17.5g
- •Fiber – 4g

GREEK SALAD

What to Use:

- •4 Persian cucumbers – chopped
- •½ cup of cherry tomatoes – quartered

- 1 small red onion – chopped finely
- ¼ cup of feta cheese (reduced fat)
- 1 tablespoon of olive oil
- 1/3 cup of Kalamata olives – halved
- 2 teaspoon of dried oregano
- Juice from 1 lemon
- Pepper
- Salt

What to Do:

- Whisk together the olive oil, oregano, pepper, salt, and lemon juice.
- In a salad bowl, combine the onions, cucumber, olives, and tomatoes. Pour the dressing on top and toss until well-combined.
- Sprinkle feta cheese on top and serve. Enjoy!

Nutrition Facts:

- Calories – 96
- Fat – 6.5g
- Carbohydrates – 7g
- Protein – 2g
- Fiber – 2.5g

SUMMER PASTA SALAD

What to Use:

- 8 ounces of whole wheat pasta
- 1 red bell pepper – diced
- 2 medium cucumbers – diced
- 1 cup of broccoli – chopped
- 4 ounces of sliced black olives – drained
- 1 small red onion – diced
- ¼ cup of mayonnaise (reduced fat)
- ½ cup of plain Greek yogurt (non-fat)

- •2 tablespoons of white vinegar
- •1 tablespoon of sugar
- •Pepper
- •Salt

What to Do:

- Cook the pasta according to its package instruction.
- Before removing the pasta add in the broccoli and cook for 45 seconds. Drain the broccoli and pasta and rinse with cold water. Transfer in a large bowl.
- Add in the onions, bell pepper, black olives, and cucumber into the bowl and toss until properly combined.
- Whisk together the mayonnaise, yogurt, vinegar, sugar, pepper, and salt. Pour dressing over the salad and toss until well-coated. Then, cover and chill until ready to serve.

Nutrition Facts:

- •Calories – 235
- •Fat – 7g
- •Carbohydrates – 36g
- •Protein – 8g
- •Fiber – 4g

PARMESAN ASPARAGUS

What to Use:

- •10 fresh asparagus spears – trimmed
- •1 tablespoon of grated parmesan cheese
- •1 tablespoon of olive oil
- •Pepper
- •Salt

What to Do:

- Turn on oven and set to 400F.

- Prepare a cookie sheet and line with aluminum foil.
- Place the asparagus spears on the cookie sheet and drizzle with olive oil. Sprinkle cheese, pepper, and salt on the asparagus and mix using hands to ensure that the vegetable is evenly coated.
- Bake for 5 minutes. Turn over the spears and bake for another 5 minutes. Remove from the oven and serve. Enjoy!

BAKED POTATO WEDGES

What to Use:

- •8 red potatoes – cut into 8 wedges
- •2 teaspoons of onion powder
- •3 tablespoons of flour
- •2 teaspoons of garlic powder
- •½ teaspoon of ground black pepper
- •1 teaspoon of seasoned salt
- •4 tablespoons of olive oil

What to Do:

- Turn on oven and set to 450F. Prepare a large baking sheet and line with tin foil. Pour the olive oil on top and spread to grease the baking sheet.
- Add the onion powder, flour, garlic powder, black pepper, and salt in a plastic bag and add a few wedges of potatoes at a time. Shake to coat the potatoes evenly. Place the potatoes on the baking sheet. Do the same with the remaining wedges.
- Bake for 20 minutes then turn the potato wedges over. Bake for another 20 minutes. Once done, sprinkle with salt if necessary. Serve while still hot. Enjoy!

SUNSHINE SALAD

What to Use:

- •16 ounces of canned mandarin oranges
- •1 pack of instant vanilla pudding mix (sugar-free and fat-free)
- •20 ounces of canned pineapple chunks

What to Do:

- Combine the mandarin oranges, pudding mix, and pineapple chunks in a bowl. Do not drain fruit juices from the can.
- Place in the refrigerator for 1 hour before serving.

Nutrition Facts:

- Calories – 94.3
- Cholesterol – 0mg
- Sodium – 2.4mg
- Carbohydrates – 24.3g
- Protein – 1g

BERRY CRISP

What to Use:

For the fruit

- 16 ounces of frozen mixed berries
- 1 teaspoon of cinnamon
- 8 ounces of vanilla pudding mix (sugar-free) – cook
- ¼ cup of milk (non-fat)
- ½ teaspoon of nutmeg

For the crisp

- 1 ½ cups of old-fashioned oats
- 8 ounces of plain yogurt (fat-free)
- ½ cup of sugar substitute
- 1 teaspoon of almond extract

What to Do:

1. Prepare an 8-inch square baking pan and grease with cooking spray.
2. Combine the mixed berries, cinnamon, pudding, milk, and nutmeg in a mixing bowl.
3. In another bowl, combine the oats, yogurt, sugar substitute, and almond extract.
4. Place the berry mixture into the baking pan and sprinkle the oat mixture on top.

5. Bake for 45 minutes at 350F. Serve while still hot. Enjoy!

Nutrition Facts:

- Calories – 121.6
- Cholesterol – 1mg
- Sodium – 34.6mg
- Carbohydrates – 22g
- Protein – 5.2g

BAR COOKIES

What to Use:

- ½ cup of unsalted butter – softened
- 3 tablespoons of water
- ½ cup of light brown sugar – packed
- 2 eggs
- 2 cups of semisweet chocolate chips
- 18 ounces of white cake mix with pudding

What to Do:

1. Turn on oven and set to 350F.
2. Prepare a 9-inch rectangular baking pan and spray with cooking spray.
3. Combine the sugar and butter and mix until fluffy and light. Add in water and eggs and mix.
4. Stir in the white cake mix. Mix until well-incorporated.
5. Stir in the chocolate chips.
6. Pour the batter into the baking pan and spread evenly at the bottom.
7. Bake in the oven for 35 minutes. Once done, cool completely before slicing into bars.

Nutrition Facts:

- Calories – 214.3
- Cholesterol – 27.8mg
- Sodium – 151.1mg

- Carbohydrates – 30.6g
- Protein – 2g

LEMON BARS

What to Use:

- 1 1/3 cups of flour
- 8 tablespoons of unsalted butter – sliced into ½-inch pieces
- 5 tablespoons of light brown sugar
- 4 large eggs
- 1 ½ cups of powdered sugar
- ½ teaspoon of vanilla extract
- ¾ cup of lemon juice

What to Do:

- Turn on oven and set to 350F.
- To make crust, combine the brown sugar and flour in a food processor. Add in butter and pulse until the mixture forms a dough-like mixture.
- Prepare a 9-inch rectangular baking pan and pack the dough at the bottom to form the crust. Bake in the oven for 20 minutes.
- To make the topping, beat eggs using an electric mixer. Add ¾ cup of powdered sugar and vanilla extract. Mix until well-incorporated. Add the remaining powdered sugar and lemon juice and mix until the sugar is dissolved completely.
- Once the crust has finished baking, lower the temperature to 300F and pour the lemon filling on top of the crust. Bake for 30 minutes.
- Once done, cool completely before cutting into 24 bars.

Nutrition Facts:

- Calories – 113.6, Cholesterol – 45.4mg, Sodium – 13.6mg
- Carbohydrates – 16.3g, Protein – 1.8g

WHOOPI PIES

What to Use:

- 1 cup of all-purpose flour
- 1 teaspoon of baking soda
- ¼ cup of unsweetened cocoa powder
- ¼ teaspoon of salt
- ¼ cup of vegetable shortening
- ½ cup of sugar
- ½ cup of 1% milk (low-fat)
- 1 egg white
- ¾ cup of marshmallow cream

What to Do:

- Mix together the cocoa, flour, salt, and baking soda.
- Beat together the egg white, shortening, and sugar using an electric mixer. Once the mixture becomes fluffy, add in the milk and flour mixture and stir until properly combined.
- Spoon a dough on a baking sheet and repeat the process until all the dough is used up.
- Bake in the oven for 7 minutes.
- Once the cookies are cool enough to handle, divide into two.
- Spread marshmallow cream on the first half of the cookies. Top with the second half. Enjoy!

Nutrition Facts:

- Calories – 109, Cholesterol – 0.3mg, Sodium – 116.3mg, Carbohydrates – 19.4g, Protein – 1.5g

Slow Cooker Beef and Barbeque

This recipe needs 10 minutes to prepare, 6 hours to cook and will make 8 servings.

Nutrition Facts:

- Protein: 25 grams
- Carbs: 17 grams
- Fats: 16.8 grams
- Saturated Fats: 1.2 grams
- Sugar: 8.7 grams
- Fiber .5 grams
- Calories: 313
- Smart Points: 9

What to Use

- Ground black pepper (to taste)
- Sea salt (to taste)
- Cayenne pepper (.25 tsp.)
- Paprika (1 tsp.)
- Garlic powder (1 tsp.)
- Onion powder (1 T)
- Worcestershire sauce (2 tsp.)
- Hot sauce (1 T)
- Brown sugar (.5 cups)
- Yellow mustard (.5 cups)
- Ketchup (1 cup)
- Apple cider vinegar (1 cup)
- Beef roast (2 lbs.)

What to Do

- Add 1 cup of water as well as the beef to a slow cooker and let them cook, covered, on a low setting for 6 hours.
- Once ingredients to Use are done cooking, discard the bones and add everything else to a blender and blend well prior to serving.
- At the 5 hour mark, start to prepare the barbeque sauce by taking a saucepan and adding gin the cayenne, paprika, garlic powder, onion powder, Worcestershire sauce, hot sauce, brown sugar, yellow mustard, ketchup and apple cider vinegar and mixing well before placing it on top of a burner over a stove set to a high heat.
- Let the sauce boil 5 minutes, regularly stirring.
- After the slow cooker, has finished cooking the beef, remove it and drain the slow cooker before adding in the beef as well as 60 percent of the sauce.
- Cook everything for 30 minutes on a high heat and top with the remaining sauce prior to serving.

Slow Cooker Stew

This recipe needs 10 minutes to prepare, 6 hours to cook and will make 4 servings.

Nutrition Facts:

- Protein: 27 grams
- Carbs: 20 grams
- Fats: 11 grams
- Saturated Fats: 3 grams
- Sugar: 3 grams
- Fiber 3 grams
- Calories: 290
- Smart Points: 7

What to Use

- Beef broth (8 cups)
- Garlic (4 cloves minced)
- Onion (1 large, chopped)
- Carrots (4 medium peeled, chopped)
- Potatoes (4 peeled, chopped)
- Chuck roast (2 lbs. beef, cubed)
- Ground black pepper (as needed)
- Sea salt (to taste)
- Celery (4 stalks chopped)

What to Do

- Add all of ingredients to Use, except for the celery to a slow cooker and let them cook, covered, on a high setting for 6 hours.
- 20 minutes before the stew is done cooking, add in the celery.
- Serve and enjoy!

Slow Cooker Tacos

This recipe needs 20 minutes to prepare, 6 hours to cook and will make 8 servings.

Nutrition Facts:

- Protein: 19 grams
- Carbs: 15 grams
- Fats: 17 grams
- Saturated Fats: 2.1 gram
- Sugar: .5 grams
- Fiber 2 grams
- Calories: 288
- Smart Points: 8

What to Use

- 6 inch tortillas (8)
- Bay leaves (2)
- Ground black pepper (to taste)
- Thyme (.25 tsp. dried)
- Cilantro (1 cup chopped)
- Cayenne pepper (.25 tsp.)
- Cinnamon (.5 tsp.)
- Cumin (.5 tsp. ground)
- Chuck roast (2 lbs. beef, cubed)
- Garlic (8 cloves minced)
- Onion (1 chopped)
- Tomatoes (2 chopped)
- 2 jalapeno peppers (chopped, seeded)
- Oil (1 T)

What to Do

- Add the oil to a skillet and place it on the stove over a burner set to a medium/high heat.
- Add in the garlic as well as the onion, tomatoes and peppers and let them cook for 5 minutes before removing them from the pan and adding them to a blender with 1 tsp. salt and .5 cups water and blend well.
- Add the results back into the skillet before mixing in the beef and turning the burner to medium and let it brown.
- Mix in the cayenne pepper, cinnamon and cumin and let everything cook for an additional minute.
- As this cooks, add 1.5 cups of water as well as the thyme and cilantro into the blender and blend well.
- Add all of ingredients to Use to the slow cooker and let them cook, covered, on a low heat for 6 hours.
- Discard the bay leaves prior to adding ingredients to Use to the tortillas and serving.

Mushrooms and Beef Noodles

This recipe needs 25 minutes to prepare, 6 hours to cook and will make 4 servings.

Nutrition Facts:

- Protein: 29 grams
- Carbs: 29 grams
- Fats: 11.8 grams
- Saturated Fats: 6.9 grams
- Sugar: 2 grams
- Fiber 1 grams
- Calories: 364
- Smart Points: 10

What to Use

- Egg noodles (2 cups cooked)
- Water (.25 cups cold)
- Cornstarch (2 T)
- Worcestershire sauce (1 T)
- Beef broth (2 cups)
- Red wine (.3 cups)
- Olive oil (2 tsp.)
- Salt (.5 tsp.)
- Beef tips (1 lb.)
- Onion (1 sliced, halved)
- Mushrooms (.5 lbs.)

What to Do

- Place the onion and the mushrooms into the slow cooker.
- Season the meet as needed before placing it, along with the oil, into a skillet before placing the skillet onto the stove on top of a burner set to a high/medium heat.
- Let the meat brown before adding it into the slow cooker.
- Ensure the skillet is deglazed before adding in the Worcestershire sauce as well as the broth and mixing well.
- Add the results to the slower cooker and let everything cook on a low heat for 6 hours.
- Combine the water and cornstarch, add the results to the slow cooker and let everything cook on high for 15 minutes.
- Plate the noodles and top with the beef tip mixture prior to serving.

Beef Ragu Style

This recipe needs 10 minutes to prepare, 8 hours to cook and will make 10 servings.

Nutrition Facts:

- Protein: 29 grams
- Carbs: 6 grams
- Fats: 9 grams
- Saturated Fats: 4 grams
- Sugar: 3 grams
- Fiber 2 grams
- Calories: 224
- Smart Points: 5

What to Use

- Thyme (2 T chopped)
- Rosemary (2 T chopped)
- Bay leaves (2)
- Beef broth (1.5 cups)
- Tomatoes (14.5 oz. crushed)
- Tomatoes (14.5 oz. diced)
- Garlic (4 cloves minced)
- Carrot (1 diced)
- Onion (.5 diced)
- Celery (1 rib diced)
- Lean been (2.5 lbs.)

What to Do

- Add all of ingredients to Use to the slow cooker before covering it, setting it to a low temperature and letting it cook for eight hours.

Lasagna Beef

This recipe needs 20 minutes to prepare, 6 hours to cook and will make 6 servings.

Nutrition Facts:

- Protein: 28 grams
- Carbs: 31 grams
- Fats: 14 grams
- Saturated Fats: 7 grams
- Sugar: 2 grams
- Fiber 1 grams
- Calories: 360
- Smart Points: 11

What to Use

- Parmesan cheese (.5 cups shredded)
- Lasagna noodles (6)
- Mozzarella cheese (1.5 cups shredded)
- Ricotta cheese (1 cup)
- Red pepper flakes (.25 tsp.)
- Basil (.5 tsp. dried)
- Oregano (1 tsp. dried)
- Salt (1 tsp.)
- Tomato sauce (15 oz.)
- Tomato (28 oz. crushed)
- Garlic (1 clove minced)
- Onion (1 chopped)
- Ground beef (1 lb.)

What to Do

- Place a skillet on the stove on top of a burner set to a high/medium heat before adding in the garlic, onion and beef and letting the beef brown.
- Add in the red pepper flakes, basil, oregano, salt, tomato sauce and crushed tomatoes and let the results simmer 5 minutes.
- Combine the mozzarella and the ricotta cheese.
- Add .3 of the total sauce from the skillet and add it to the slow cooker. Place 3 noodles on top of the sauce, followed by cheese mixture. Create three layers total.
- Cover the slow cooker and let it cook on a low heat for 6 hours.

Beef Chili

This recipe needs 20 minutes to prepare, 5 hours to cook and will make 12 servings.

Nutrition Facts:

- Protein: 13 grams
- Carbs: 17 grams
- Fats: 3 grams
- Saturated Fats: 1 grams
- Sugar: 2 grams
- Fiber 5 grams
- Calories: 138
- Smart Points: 4

What to Use

- Ground black pepper (to taste)
- Sea salt (to taste)
- Tomato paste (2 T)
- Green chilies (.25 cups diced)
- Sweet onion (1 chopped)
- Kidney beans (15 oz. rinsed, drained)
- Tomatoes (28 oz. crushed)
- Cumin (2 tsp.)
- Chili powder (2 T)
- Green bell pepper (1 diced, seeded)
- Red bell pepper (1 diced, seeded)
- Garlic (1 T minced)
- Ground beef (1 lb.)

What to Do

- Place a skillet on the stove on top of a burner set to a high/medium heat before adding in the garlic, onion and beef and letting the beef brown.
- Drain the fat from the pan and return the meet to it before adding in the bell peppers and cooking for 5 minutes prior to seasoning using the cumin and chili powder.
- Add the tomato paste, green chilies, onion, kidney beans, tomatoes and meat mix into the slow cooker and mix well. Cook on high, covered for 5 hours.
- Season to taste prior to serving.

Beef Stroganoff

This recipe needs 5 minutes to prepare, 6 hours to cook and will make 6 servings.

Nutrition Facts:

- Protein: 20 grams
- Carbs: 15 grams
- Fats: 8 grams
- Saturated Fats: 3 grams
- Sugar: 6 grams
- Fiber 0 grams
- Calories: 216
- Smart Points: 7

What to Use

- Ground black pepper (to taste)
- Sea salt (to taste)
- Onion soup mix (1.25 oz.)
- Sour cream (16 oz.)
- Cream of mushroom soup (10.75 oz.)
- Ground beef (1 lb.)

What to Do

- Place a skillet on the stove on top of a burner set to a high/medium heat before adding in the garlic, onion and beef and letting the beef brown.
- Add the beef into the slow cooker before combining the other Ingredients Use in a bowl and then adding them in on top.
- Cover the slow cooker and let it cook on a low heat for 6 hours.

Beef Burgundy

This recipe needs 15 minutes to prepare, 6 hours to cook and will make 6 servings.

Nutrition Facts:

- Protein: 12 grams
- Carbs: 42 grams
- Fats: 9 grams
- Saturated Fats: 3.2 grams
- Sugar: 7 grams
- Fiber 0 grams
- Calories: 324
- Smart Points: 13

What to Use

- Ground black pepper (to taste)
- Sea salt (to taste)
- Egg noodles (3 cups cooked)
- Bay leaf (1)
- Mushroom (8 oz. sliced)
- Thyme (.5 tsp.)
- Onion (16 oz. chopped)
- Tomato paste (2 T)

- Red win e(.5 cups)
- Beef broth (10 oz.)
- All-purpose flour (.3 cups)
- Garlic (1 clove minced)
- Round steak (2 lbs. cubed)

What to Do

- Place a skillet on the stove on top of a burner set to a high/medium heat. Add in the steak and let it brown before adding it to the slow cooking.
- Add the garlic and onion to the skillet and coat the skillet using cooking spray before letting them cook 5 minutes. Add in the flour and cook an additional minute.
- Add the rest of ingredients to Use to the skillet before adding it all to the slow cooker. Cover the slow cooker, turn it to a high heat and let it cook for an hour prior to turning the heat to low and cooking an additional 5 hours.
- Remove the bay leaf and serve with the egg noodles.

The Bonus 7 Step Action

1.The Ultimate weight loss program

Everyone who wants to lose weight has probably tried multiple diets, supplements and/or plans. There are hundreds of weight loss methods available to buy. All of them making wild promises.

There are no magical pills, diets or exercise gadgets that will make weight instantly disappear. It comes down to eating right, staying healthy and burning more calories than you take in.

That is where the saying "calories in - calories out" comes from. You want to make sure you burn more calories (out) than you consume (in).

Clearly, this is a simplistic view and a proper diet consists of taking more than calories into consideration. We will look at that in other chapters, but right now we want to talk about creating a calorie deficit.

In order to track this you need some basic information. First off you need to figure out how many calories you burn per day naturally. This comes down to factors such as age and weight.

Calculating Number of Calories You Burn Daily

For Men: 66 + (12.7 x height in inches) + (6.23 x weight in pounds) - (6.8 x age in years).

For women: 655 + (4.7 x height in inches) + (4.35 x weight in pounds) - (4.7 x age in years).

This formula will give you the basic calories you burn daily, just by breathing, hearth pumping and etc... These are how many calories you burn if you didn't move all day (basal metabolic rate).

Once you have that number, you need to start tracking the calories you burn and the calories you consume. This can be tricky because it is a lot of information to keep track of.

This is one of the more popular calorie counters out there since it is free. It will help you track what you eat, and what you expend. You just have to enter the foods and activity you had for the day. It will even allow you to input your basal metabolic rate.

It is ideal if you can keep a daily caloric deficit, but that isn't always possible. Sometimes we slip and sometimes we indulge. If you can get a weekly caloric deficit that will still have you losing weight.

This isn't about starving yourself, or exercising until you are dead. It is all about being aware what you put in your body, and what you exert. Weight loss can be a struggle, but if you can manage your calories in and calories out - you can overcome! 2. Get Into Action

The last lesson we told you that one of the biggest factors in your weight loss journey was creating a caloric deficit. The only way you can achieve this is by getting active.

For some of us, that can be difficult. We will look for any excuse to avoid it. That is why instant diets and pill solutions are so popular. The idea of losing weight while doing nothing is very appealing.

The fact is, if you want to lose weight and more importantly keep it off - you have to get active. This is what people mean when they say weight loss is a lifestyle change. There is no excuse not to get the proper exercise. You have to burn calories and the more active you are, the more you will burn.

You don't need to join a gym. Take up a sport and have some fun. Run or walk around the neighborhood. Find some at home exercises you can do. The internet is full of them, part of this series even includes a 7 exercise booklet that you can easily perform at home, with no added equipment.

The Centers for Disease Control and Prevention states that people need (minimum):

> *150 **minutes** per week of moderate-intensity aerobic activity (such as brisk walking, riding a bike on level ground, or pushing a lawn mower) or 75 **minutes** per week of high-intensity aerobic exercise (such as running, jogging, riding a bike up hills or fast on level ground, swimming laps, or playing high-energy sports such as basketball or singles tennis)*

> *At least two sessions per week of strength training exercises such as lifting weights, working with resistance bands, engaging in strenuous functional activities like shoveling dirt, or doing exercises that use body weight (push-ups, pull-ups, squats, lunges, sit-ups, etc.)*

If you want to lose weight you have to beat that number, and beat it consistently. It does give you a great number to shoot for though, and shows you what minimums healthy people should aim for.

Exercise, regardless of type can affect a person's overall health and improves their quality of life. People should think about three things when exercising.

1) What type of exercise should I do?

2) Mild Exercise versus Moderate exercise versus Extreme exercise

3) Short programs versus Long programs

There is no evidence in support of one weight loss exercise type over another but there is no doubt that a person will not learn a way that shows them how to lose weight fast without exercise and pills and the essence is that if you wish to lose weight you have to pick one, aerobic or resistance training, and start exercising.

A program that combines both kinds of exercise can provide the most benefits. It is sometimes the most effective way for a person to get fit and trim. A person will lose weight and tone their muscles. A good regimen will have some days devoted to aerobic and some days devoted to strength training. The various programs will also help alleviate some of the boredom associated with working out. Committing to a fitness regimen is the most difficult thing that the individual must face.

What is the proper length of a workout? Longer is better. People are different and there is no set amount of time that is best for a person, but rather it is about what type of shape a person is in to begin with that decides how much they should work out. In order for someone to get into shape they should plan on exercising four days out of the week. It should be a part of your lifestyle. The need to exercise is still there when you have achieved the goals that you want. If a person quits exercising they will be back where they started.

How intense? Mild shows improvement in health at all ages and all conditions, moderately is far greater at improving health than mild, and strenuous only benefits younger and healthy people and any intensity is better than none because there is no truth to the programs that promise to show you how to lose weight fast without exercise. There is evidence that a less vigorous workout is able to give some benefits to a person who was not getting any workouts at all.

30 minutes per day of weight loss workout will keep most individuals from gaining the additional weight related with inactivity. There is no secret method to losing weight and getting a toned body and although you might see an infomercial for a product that promises to teach you how to lose weight fast at home in a week there is no replacing the old fashioned method of following a proper diet and getting regular exercise.

No exercise regimen should be started if you have not checked with your doctor first. A doctor can let a person know what is safe for them to do and can suggest ways to make their fitness regimen even better.

If you overdo it, you could hurt yourself. When you are injured, you might not be able to exercise at all. If a person limits their activities to what they are able to do they will be able to gradually up the intensity without harming their body. Limited activity is better than no activity at all.

The last part of any exercise program is motivation. You have to have a reason or working out. Motivation will provide you with the push that you need some days. It is easy to come up with excuses not to succeed if you are not committed to doing it. Find a program that you enjoy. Your goals should be about you and not anyone else. After that, give it a good effort. Once you accomplish that, you can accomplish anything.

There are many ways in which you can benefit from healthy weight loss. The fact that you are dropping ghost towns slowly means that you have a better chance at keeping them off. That isn't the case with others who go on crash diets and lose a considerable amount of weight in a very short period of time. So, how is this all possible and how do you do it successfully?

For starters, you have to understand that it is really a simple thing to accomplish. The difficult thing is making the decision and committing to it. Wouldn't it be great to lose weight and still enjoy all the foods that you love? It's possible the only differences reducing your portion sizes and the calories consumed each day.

How? Just by changing your diet! You can enjoy the foods that you love, as long as they are cooked in a different manner. If you're avoiding deep fried foods and all those extra calories in the preparation, you can see a huge improvement in the way you look and the way you feel. Do yourself a favor and pick up cookbooks that are designed with health in mind.

Of course, you can never successfully lose weight and keep it off if you aren't going to implement some kind of exercise regime into your lifestyle. Certainly, you must get your doctor's approval before you start. However, once he gives you the green light, make the commitment to stay true to it.

Many people hate the exercising part of the whole deal. But the problem with that is that with regards to diet alone, you only lose so much. Then, you will definitely plateau. Additionally, you'll probably end up somewhat unhappy because of the loose skin that has developed since the fat was lost.

Therefore, exercise is crucial. And with your exercise, you must make sure that you get a cardio workout as well.

There is nothing else really to be said. If you want to lose weight you have to make physical activity a part of your daily routine.

3. Persistent

I don't even like to think about the word sometimes. Especially when it comes to weight loss. What kills a diet more quickly than a single slip?

If you want to commit to losing weight, then you need to be able to persist through failure. Everyone who has accomplished something of note has struggled with failure at one or more points in their ascent. The difference is they persisted through it and learned a lesson.

Those is the two keys in dealing with failure. You must persist and learn.

If you slip on your diet, or miss a day of exercise, don't fret about it. Don't let it derail you. Push it from your mind. Focus on all your positive days, not the one slip up. Picture yourself at your goal weight, not in the act of devouring that donut you shouldn't have. Treat it as a cheat day and move on. This is how you persist, failing for a day is OK, just don't let that day stretch into a week and then a month.

You have to accept failures as natural and develop a tougher skin to deal with them.

The second step is to learn from your mistakes. Quite often learning from your mistakes will be more efficient than learning from your successes. When you fail, treat it as a lesson learned. It is just like in business, when you fail at something, you learn the things that don't work. This is the same with weight loss. If you have slipped off your new diet every time you drink, then maybe you avoid drinking. If you realize that every Friday you miss out on exercise because of a late work meeting then reschedule your workout.

Failure is natural part of life, along with death and taxes. You can't avoid it, and even if you could you wouldn't want to. Your life's lessons are learned through your failures along with your successes. Don't fear failure, persist through and learn from it.

4. Find A Good Partner

One of the best things you can do when you are trying to lose weight is to add some accountability to your routine. How do you do that?

The buddy system.

Having a buddy to try and lose weight with is a great motivator. You will feel more accountable to reach your weight loss goals when you are actually sharing them with someone. They can also be helpful because it is someone that can relate to you about struggling to lose weight. You can share your triumphs in joy, and your setbacks in support.

If you are working out regularly a buddy is invaluable. They can change a boring walk or jog into an exercise slash therapy session. A hike in the wilderness is always more fun with a friend along! If you are into weight lifting it is also nice to have a buddy. You guys can challenge each other while at the same time providing encouragement and practical help like spots on heavy lifts.

It is sad to say but in this day and age, you can probably find yourself a weight loss buddy in your group of friends. If you can't, don't panic you can always do it virtually as well. You could find a friend on Facebook that is losing weight and work with them. Having Facebook chats and sharing progress pictures on Facebook.

There are also web forums and sites dedicated to linking weight loss partners up virtually.

The bottom line is this - if you want to lose weight working with a friend can provide motivation, support as well as the always important accountability. Find your weight loss buddy now!

4. Tracking Results

Just like you track your calories you should track your progress for both exercise AND eating.

Tracking this info isn't meant to be a punishment, it is actually motivation! If you track all of your physical activity you will be able to look back at all you have accomplished. When you have those mornings where you feel like you just CAN'T exercise, check out your progress and take in all that you have done. It will get you out and active. If you have a calendar and you put a red X through every day that you got enough physical activity, you will want to keep that streak alive. It seems like such an old fashioned tip, but our minds work like that. We will want to keep the streak of X's going as long as possible.

You can also see the improvements. If you are working out with weights, keep track of how much weight you are lifting. It is a great feeling to watch those numbers climb. You can do the same with running, keep trying to outdistance yourself each day.

Keeping track of your workout progress could even help you diagnose problems. If you notice there are certain days that are danger areas for you, then you can figure out what happens on those days that throws you off. Just figure out the things that only happen on those days, do you see any patterns?

Tracking progress is a nice step for your nutrition too. One of the easiest ways to do that is using the calorie counting tip from the first lesson.

If you are looking for something visual you can do something like the calendar trick but related to nutrition. Every day you eat right you put an X.

Tracking progress is a great step in any weight loss program. It helps you visualize everything you have accomplished, makes it easier to diagnose negative patterns and motivates you to keep on track.

5. Eating Clean

We have talked about calories in calories out - the basic weight loss guideline. It is a basic tip because you still want to make sure you are getting those calories from good sources. Keeping your calories down by eating two corn-dogs a day probably isn't your best choice.

Eating clean is a term that doesn't have an official term but in general it means:

Eating healthy whole foods while avoiding processed foods and refined sugars.

That is a general goal to strive for, it isn't always possible to eat completely "clean" but if you are getting the majority of your calories from clean sources then you are doing great. When you eat clean you avoid processed foods so automatically things like fast food and junk food are eliminated from your diet. If you do eat some processed food don't fret over it, the idea is to eat leanly as much as possible.

Here are some general clean eating tips:

- Learn to read labels! Read the nutritional information and what to Use of everything you buy.
- Choose while grains when possible. Whole wheat doesn't necessarily mean whole grain either! Look for bread, pasta and etc... that are made with 100% whole grains
- Eat lots of fruits and vegetables. They are great whole sources of clean calories
- Prepare more of your own meals, don't eat out as much or buy microwaveable type meals. These meals even when "healthy", can be loaded with things like sodium.
- Choose lean meats when cooking. Eating meat is fine and the protein will help build muscle and make you feel full.
- Chicken and fish are great meat choices.
- Avoid processed meats like bologna or hot dogs.
- Replace junk food with unsalted or lightly salted whole nuts.
- Check out the internet for great clean recipes. Keep a list!
- Don't fret over falling off the wagon, even grat yourself a cheat day now and then.
- Eating clean while out can be tough but more restaurants are offering clean menu items. A Salad can be a good choice, but if you are really hungry you might need to add some protein!
- Start as soon as possible!

Eating clean is a great way to make sure you not only lose weight but you are overall healthy. It isn't necessarily an easy transition and you don't have to try and turn on a switch and do it overnight. If you are committed to losing weight and being healthy, you should choose to clean up your diet.

6. How Much Should You Eat?

Anyone who is trying to lose weight needs to consider their portion control. Just talk to anyone who has actually lost weight (and sustained it). They will almost assuredly bring up portion control as one of the keys for their success.

What is Portion Control?

Portion control is understanding how much a serving size is and how many calories a serving contains. One of the biggest problems overweight people face is realizing what constitutes a proper portion of food. When you eat a meal you need to realize what constitutes a serving size of your foods. While not scientific, the following list gives you an idea of some recommended portion sizes. If you struggle with weight loss, these portions might seem smaller than you thought:

- Vegetables or fruit is about the size of your fist.
- Pasta is about the size of one scoop of ice cream.
- Meat, fish, or poultry is the size of a deck of cards or the size of your palm (minus the fingers).
- Snacks such as pretzels and nuts are about the size of a cupped handful.
- Potato is the size of a computer mouse.
- Steamed rice is the size of a cupcake wrapper.
- Cheese is the size of a pair of dice or the size of your whole thumb (from the tip to the base).

I know personally that the cheese serving size surprised me when I first saw it. You can find portion information online. You can find much more specific portion control guides online as well. Some sites will break it down by food weight, so you may need to weight your food for exact portions. The above list though is good enough to give you a rough idea.

When you eat a meal, control your portions! Learning how much food you actually need is one of the biggest steps you will take on your weight loss journey.

7. Positive Image

Many of the tips in this guide are specific. You need to eat less, exercise more, control portions etc... Those are all very valuable tips and will help you immensely. This tip is more cerebral. Much like tip #3 - Persist through Failure, this tip is more about your state of mind.

A person's personality, attitude and state of mind is just as important as the exercise and portion control in my opinion. Of course, eating less and exercising more is the key, but how do you get in the right mood to accomplish that? You have to train your mind along with your body, or you will never sustain weight loss.

Visualization is an amazing tool for motivating yourself, and keeping that motivation high at all times.

By definition visualization is:

A technique involving focusing on positive mental images in order to achieve a particular goal

No matter what goal you want to accomplish visualization can help. It will help keep you motivated, as well as potentially train your subconscious to work with you rather than against you.

Some visualization tips include:

- Envision your ideal body in your mind everyday.

- Envision all of the great activities you will do with your new boy.

- Envision how it will feel to shop for normal clothes

- Envision how people will treat you differently.

- A great time to visualize is before bed or when waking up. Spend 10 minutes doing visualization as often as you can.

- Create a vision board! Post pictures of healthy foods and physiques on a cork board that you have in your office or house.

- Change your desktop background to an edited picture that is your head on a healthy body. Every time you sit at your computer you will see it and be motivated!

Visualization isn't some magic pill. It won't let you lose weight on its own. It isn't some fairy tale either. There is science to prove that visualization helps improve results and keep you motivated. All high achievers visualize there success.

Visualization can help with any of your goals, and since weight loss can be one of the most important, there is no reason to not use it. Visualize your future body to stay motivated.

Activities Workout Routine

This guide is designed to show you one new calorie burning exercise per day. We have broken the guide down like that for ease of training. The exercises are probably familiar to you but the classic exercises are just that for a reason - they work and they are easy.

Each day we introduce a new exercise. Once introduced you should use it the following days as well. Eventually at the end of the week you will be doing each exercise everyday.

It will be your daily 7 Exercise routine.

This workout is low impact enough that you can do it everyday, but that is up to you. The more you do it the better the results.

If you want to make any of these exercises more challenging, simply raise the reps or sets. A rep is doing the exercise once, while a set is a number of those reps. You can also add weights to make some of the exercises tougher.

Please consult your doctor before you take on any new training regimen.

Calories burned are approximated and can swing wildly depending on things like current weight and other circumstances. Monday - Power Walk

This is one of the easiest activities to add to your daily routine.

Barring a disability, most of us walk everyday. We have grown up walking, jogging and running. Most times people start exercising by walking and or running. That is often the only exercise people do.

This is because it is easy and effective.

You can do this inside on a treadmill, but I suggest outside. The varied terrain and wind resistance will make for a better exercise. It is also mentally soothing to go for a walk outside.

This is not a casual stroll though, you will want to keep your pace up on this walk. If power walk is too tame for you, you can also jog or run.

How To & Tips

In power walking posture counts. Stand up straight as possible. This will allow all your muscles through the core to work together and it will help you walk faster.

Look ahead not down.

Relax Shoulders

Walk with your arms close to body and a 90 degree angle at the elbow.

Stride forward at a brisk pace you can handle, your heel should be striking the ground first.

Wear firm soled comfortable shoes. Power walking shoes are preferred.

Duration: 20 Minutes
Calories Burned: ~300

Tuesday - Triangle Push Up

The triangle push up is a variation of the push up most of us are familiar with. This simple variation will work more muscles in your upper body.

I would do this exercise after the power walk personally. The power walk will have your blood flowing and make you more receptive to this muscle building exercise.

This push up is just like the normal push up except that you bring your hands in so your thumbs and pointer fingers are forming a triangle.

How To & Tips

Kneel face down.
Place your hands on the floor and position them below your chest with your thumbs and pointer fingers close enough to form a triangle.
Stretch out into normal push up position, parallel to the ground.
Lower yourself down near ground level and then push yourself up again to complete one push up.
If you cannot complete this motion, then you can keep your knees on the ground until you have built up enough arm strength to do the full version.
To complete a full set do 10 pushups with no break in between.
Do three of these sets.

Duration: 3 Sets of 10
Calories Burned: ~75

Here is a video showing how to do the push up:

https://www.youtube.com/watch?v=iY3CZ01lR0w

And Here

https://www.youtube.com/watch?v=aSxTKvSP3bc

Wednesday - Body Weight Squat

This is one of the most popular exercises for serious weight trainers. While they do theirs with huge weights on their back, this body weight only version is still effective.

A squat works primarily your legs, but the amazing thing is it also works man other muscles in your body. Weight trainers refer to this exercise as a true full body workout.

Learning the body weight squat is usually suggested before you move onto weighted squats.

The squat is basically done from the standing position, and you squat down towards the ground, in a sitting motion. Then you finish the squat by standing back up straight.

If you don't find the body weight squats challenging enough, then add dumbbells in each of your hands. Make sure to have the same weight on each side.

How To & Tips

Stand up with your feet a little more than shoulder width apart, toes pointed 30 degrees out.
Squat down into a sitting like position.
Squat as far as you are comfortable with.
Some people squat until their thighs are parallel with ground, others like the slightly break that plane.
Don't risk your form for speed. Keeping the proper form is more important than finishing quickly.
Squatting down and then back up is a rep.
A set is 10 reps.

Duration: 3 Sets of 10

Calories Burned: ~105

Here is 1 variation of the body squat

Thursday - The Curl-Up

Another variation on a classic exercise. This exercise is based on the sit-up which is one of the first exercises you will learn along with running and pushups. This exercise burns calories, while working the abdominal and other core muscles.

This exercise is slightly different than a sit-up or crunch. Some studies have shown it causes less impact on the lower back. The exercise is essentially a crunch, but the arms stay at the side of the body. This is to protect the neck and back muscles.

One rep is a curl up and then back down onto the mat.

How To & Tips

Lie down on your back, if you have an exercise or yoga mat, use that.

Place your hands at your sides, arms straight forward and on the mat or ground.

Contract your abs, curl up as if you were doing a crunch moving your hands along the ground towards your heels. Keep your head up.

Return to the starting point and that is one rep.

Duration: 3 Sets of 10

Calories Burned: **~75Friday - Shadow Boxing**

It is estimated that people are 38% more likely to stick with a new exercise if they find it fun or enjoyable. It makes sense that you would find it easier to do a task that you actually find fun this is why shadow boxing is a great exercise.

It is not just for combat sports enthusiasts either. Shadow boxing is a good aerobic workout, easy to do and somewhat therapeutic. This exercise not only works your body, it can help soothe your mind. It provides a great outlet for your day's frustrations.

If you want to up the resistance in the exercise and make it more challenging you can add weights to your hands, or use a heavy bag with boxing gloves.

How To & Tips

Great thing about shadow boxing is it isn't as form dependent as other exercises.

Stand comfortably. Hold your hands up, making a tight fist with your thumb tight against the outside of your fingers.

Do not tuck your thumb inside fingers, if you accidentally hit something your thumb could be injured.

Keep your elbows close to your body and your chin tucked down

Throw some punches as if you were boxing.

Start throwing a couple jabs and then work up in speed as the exercise progresses.

While punching you should be moving around, keep on the balls of your feet.

Remember to use head movement and lean back and forth as if you were avoiding punches from an opponent.

Have fun!

Duration: 15 Minutes (one minute break 2x in there)

Calories Burned: ~105

Saturday Dips

This exercise burns calories as well as builds muscle. This is one of the best body weight work outs for your arms. This is an exercise you will probably feel in your arms a day (or more likely 2) after you have done it.

This exercise can be done a couple different ways, but in general using two a dining room chair is perfect. Like most exercises in this book, this exercise is so convenient you could do it in a hotel room on a business trip. It just takes your own body weight and a chair.

The general idea is that you raise your own body weight with just your arms.

How To & Tips

Stand in front of a chair, facing away from it.

Sit down on the very edge of the chair.

Place your hands so they are on the edge of the chair about shoulder width apart.

Make sure your hands are secured and slide your butt of the edge of the chair, walking out with your feet. Keep your chest and head up.

Slowly lower your body downward. Don't bend your elbows past 90 degrees.

Now push your body back up by extending your arms.

Lowering down and then raising up constitutes one rep.

If 3 sets of 8 reps is too much start out with one set and work your way up.

If you find this exercise too easy, an advanced dip can be performed by resting your feet on edge of another chair.

Duration: 3 Sets of 8
Calories Burned: ~75

Sunday - Power Jumps

We saved this exercise for the last day because it is a great way to wind down your days activities. It is one last explosive body weight exercise to finish your routine out.

You will want to make sure you have room to do this exercise, and are on a firm floor. You probably don't want to jump around anything fragile or that could fall off a shelf. The key to this exercise is using your core muscles to explode, you don't want to hold back on the jumps because you are scared of knocking something over. If it is a nice day this is a great exercise to get out into the yard and do.

It is pretty easy to do, since most of us have been jumping since were kids. If you want to add difficulty the exercise, hold some light dumbbells in each hand (same weight).

How To & Tips

Find somewhere you are comfortable jumping as high as possible.

Stand up with your knees slightly bent and your feet close together.

Bend down then jump straight up as high as you can.

Land with your knees loose to absorb impact.

As you land go into a squat position and then explode into your next jump as you rise up.

One jump is one rep.

Read the squat lesson from Wednesday to figure out what a squat position is

Duration: 3 Sets of 10

Calories Burned: ~125

You now have a 7 exercise routine that you can use at any times. If you feel like the workout is too strenuous break it up so you do 3 one day and 4 the next. Ideally though you would like to perform all 7 activities per day.

You can also break up the activities throughout the day. You could take your power walk first thing each morning, and then do a couple of the other exercises each time you take a break. These are the perfect exercises for people who stay or work from home as well.

A very rough approximation is that going through all of these exercises will burn 900 calories. This number can vary wildly based on gender, and body weight and level of exertion.

Conclusion

Losing weight isn't an easy task. It takes hard work and time. If you use the tips in the guide you will begin to see results much sooner than you think.

I hope this book was able to help you to achieve your fitness goals through these amazingly delicious recipes.

The next step is to take your diet to the next level and create a meal plan using these recipes. By creating your own meals, you'll gradually learn how to choose healthier food alternatives and re-create other recipes to fit into your diet

Follow the tips in this guide, and your weight loss journey will be off to a great start.

Congratulation and good life to all who read this book.

Made in the USA
Middletown, DE
21 June 2019